Cheating Death, Living Life

- Linda's story

Ralph Turner
with Linda Huskisson

RIVER
PUBLISHING

River Publishing & Media Ltd
Barham Court
Teston
Maidstone
Kent
ME18 5BZ
United Kingdom

info@river-publishing.co.uk

ISBN 978-1-908393-36-4
Printed in the United Kingdom
Cover design by www.SpiffingCovers.com

By the same author:
Working for God
GOD-Life

Contents

What Others Are Saying...   4

Dedication   9

Acknowledgements   11

Author's note   12

Foreword   13

Introduction   15

Chapter 1 – Running Before I Was Born   17

Chapter 2 – Left For Dead   31

Chapter 3 – "Mummy, Come Home."   41

Chapter 4 – "Just 10 Minutes, Love."   51

Chapter 5 – Modern Slavery   59

Chapter 6 – All The Time In The World   69

Chapter 7 – The Man In The Night   79

Chapter 8 – All You Have To Do Is Ask   89

Chapter 9 – The God Who Answers Prayer   99

Chapter 10 – Six Months To Live   109

Chapter 11 – A Past And A Future   119

A Letter From Linda   133

About the Author   135

What Others Are Saying About This Book...

'Having known Linda for many years, she truly is a trophy of grace; a life transformed by the power of God's love. Her honesty to allow Father God to shape her and change her has been a tremendous blessing to many people. Through the Celebrate Recovery course Linda's story continues to help others into freedom today. I believe this book will bring hope to many who have no hope.'

– **Janie Bingham**, Community Work Pastor, KingsGate Community Church

'*Cheating Death, Living Life* is a powerful testimony to the life-changing grace of God. It makes a compelling read! The description of Linda's abusive past, the drug addiction, the prostitution, the beatings; in all it's a brutal and painful reality.

But it gives way to her experience of God's forgiveness and miraculous healing. It's like the bright rays of a new day after the dark of a stormy night. Ralph Turner has done an excellent job of sharing her story. May it impart hope, faith and the unconditional love of God to everyone who reads it.

Thank you Linda for sharing your story with the world. And thank you Jesus, for your amazing grace!'

– **Jonathan Conrathe**, Founder, Mission24

'So many people will read Linda's life story and identify with some of the sadness and hopelessness in their own lives. When Jesus comes into a life He changes it dramatically, miraculously,

and for eternity. You will be blessed and amazed by Linda's story. Your life can be changed for all time too. Thank you Jesus!'
— **Keith Crump**, Senior Pastor, Crawley Community Church

'Slavery is real and living in your neighbourhood. This story should galvanise you to stand up and become part of the solution. If we're apathetic we're part of the problem. This story has inspired me to do more to bring hope back to those who have had it taken from them.'
— **John Draper**, Partnerships Director, Compassion UK

'This story grips the reader from beginning to end. You just have to keep reading to find out what happens next. A roller coaster of a life from pillar to post ... until it finally comes to land and the reader can breathe at last.

How can God persist with such a person? A woman who is controlled by men, drugs and a lifestyle she'd never have chosen. She ended up with a storm whichever way she turned until God's people met her, persisted in their contact with her and well, readers will have to read it themselves and find the God who transforms lives! A 'Nicky Cruz' style story, but British and more recent!'
— **Dr Anne E. Dyer**, Lecturer, Mattersey Hall Christian College

'This book is compelling reading for everyone, showing the love of God for His creation and the grace He so freely bestows on us as we call upon Him. A must read.'
— **Pastors Will and Barbara Graham**, Victory Christian Centre, Rugeley

'Linda's story is a gripping, page-turning "read it in one sitting" story of the overwhelming grace of God in Jesus. It reads like it's straight off the pages of the New Testament. I felt like I was meeting the woman from Simon the Pharisee's house in Luke 7 face to face.'

—**Dr Andy Johnston**, Pastor, ChristChurch Hailsham, Newfrontiers

'Paul says in the Bible, "I am not ashamed of the Gospel, because it is the power of God for the salvation of everyone who believes..." I am ashamed of the brutes who abuse their wives and their children; of the pimps who traffic vulnerable young men and women; of the dealers who use substance abuse to control their victims.

But the good news is that the Gospel of Jesus can triumph over it all. Ralph has done a great job of bringing Linda's story to a wider audience. Thank you Linda; thank you Ralph.'

— **Peter Lyne**, author *Baton Change – The Next Generation* and *First Apostles, Last Apostles*

'Be prepared, this story tells of some dark places in life. For some, this is the world they live in; isolated, lonely and painful. The book prompts us to care; it reminds us of a persistent loving Jesus. You will learn of Linda, an overcomer, a modern day miracle finder, a responder to the heart, voice and call of God. Her story is one of a living Saviour, who cares, who has changed her life and who has replaced her many tears with laughter, hope and joy. I pray her story makes a difference to you; it has the power to do so.'

— **Steven Pettican**, Co-Founder, Network Peterborough

'Thank you Linda for having the courage to tell the inspiring story of your journey to faith in Jesus Christ. Keep shining with His love and light!'
– **Karen Smith**, Co-Founder, KingsGate Community Church

'This page-turner will affect you profoundly; a real life story of tragedy then redemption. The depths of pain are matched only by the grace of a God who is able to stretch out His hand to heal and perform miracles in even the most abused and broken of hearts and bodies. This book will help everyone – for the privileged: compassion; for doubters: faith; for those of us working with the abused, oppressed and addicted: encouragement; and for those in the depths of darkness: hope.'
– **Ed Walker**, Founder and Director, Hope into Action

'When you realise you're at the bottom, the only way is up. Bearing a weight that would cripple most, Linda needed more than a little 'hand-up'. What she found was amazing forgiveness and received amazing grace. Linda's is a story of astonishing transformation to warm the soul and bring praise to an awesome, loving, God.'
– **Peter Walker**, National Director of The Leprosy Mission, (Formerly, Executive Director of Prison Fellowship)

Dedication

This book is dedicated to any who have lost hope.

There is a way out.

There is always a hope and a future.

Acknowledgements

From Linda...

Well, all I can say is, 'Well done, Ralph and Roh!' A huge thank you for all your hard work. I didn't think my testimony was easy, but you took on the challenge and made it great. May God continue to bless you in writing books that can influence other people's lives. May God continue to bless you in your ministry.

I would like to say a big thank you to my husband, Ricky. I know it hasn't always been easy, but I can honestly say I love you more today than I ever have. God certainly gave me the best when I cried out for a husband. You were hand-picked by God and we have never looked back.

I also want to pay tribute to my children and grandchildren and say a big thank you for inviting us into your lives. I love you all so much and am very proud of you. To my brothers and their families, thank you for your support through the good times and the bad.

Thank you to Dave and Karen Smith and the family I have found at KingsGate Community Church. It is a privilege and an honour to serve in our church. I would also like to thank Janie Bingham, who has had a great influence in my life. You have such a caring and pastoral heart.

Thank you to my friends who have shaped my life. Many of you appear in the pages of this book. Toni and Karen, thank you for rescuing me. Alethea, thank you for believing in me.

I want to honour God in this book. He so deserves it! If I had chosen not to follow Jesus I would be dead. It's as simple as that. It's because of God's love and grace that I am here to tell the tale. 'The old life is gone; a new life has begun!' (2 Corinthians 5:17 NLT)

From Ralph...

A big thank you to my wife, Roh, for all the encouragement, interview help and proof reading. Thanks to Ali Parkes and Pauline Stevens for their proof reading – what a labour of love! Thank you to Tim Pettingale and River Publishing for all the support.

My love and appreciation as always to my family: Roh, Nathan and Joy, Elspeth, Rob and Jessica, Josh and Lois.

Thank you to everyone in the KingsGate family. I'm so grateful to be part of a church that is transforming lives from our neighbourhoods to the nations by the power of God's love.

And thank you, Linda, for your bravery in telling your story.

Author's Note:

I have written this book in the first person, as if Linda was telling the story. And really, she is. The book was written off the back of copious notes and interviews over the last two years. I hope I have captured not only the story, but the way Linda thinks and talks. However, you will need to be the judge of that!

Please note that some of the names have been changed in this book in order to protect the person's identity where necessary.
–*Ralph Turner*

Foreword

Transformation is a big word. Increasingly, it is occupying the thoughts of Bible scholars and academics, NGO specialists and strategic thinkers in mission agencies and pastors.

And it's all really good news. Talk of transformation is another way in which the Christian church is coming to review its mission in the world: not merely as people called out to survive the 21st century, but as communities of healing who, through words and deeds, initiate change and bring hope to countless multitudes across the world through preaching and practising kindness.

The idea that people and communities can be changed has been packaged and commodified. To help us on this journey, we have devised conferences, teaching tools, theories and theologies to make better sense of the expansive idea of transformation.

But every so often, a story comes along which is powerful because it's simple. And it is authentic because it demonstrates

God's ability to change us as He rescues us from overwhelmingly complicated webs of entanglements we weave about us, through our circumstances and our choices in response to those situations.

This is Linda's story: the life of a woman who found forgiveness and cheated death. I know a little of this great pilgrimage, having met Linda in the criminal justice system during those darker days, as she passed through the shadows of death. I knew the pre-transformed Linda in the days of prison and dysfunctionality, when her potential for change was overwhelmed by her circumstances. And I began to see in her the possibility of transformation.

So imagine my delight and amazement when, after some years, a new Linda found me in order to tell me her story of transformation. A new woman living life.

Linda's exciting story is what transformation looks like. Read it and remember that God is still changing lives in the world today.

Rev Joel Edwards

International Director, Micah Challenge

Introduction

It felt unreal.

There was a strength in my body I'd not known for many years. Just a prayer. That's all it had been.

Slowly, very slowly, I eased myself out of the hospital bed and into a standing position. No pain. A few minutes before I'd been doubled over, but now, here I was, standing straight.

It was impulsive – reaching for the vase of flowers, I took out the biggest, the most beautiful. Carefully cradling the yellow petals, I began to walk. Out of the ward. Down the corridor. Through to the chapel. There, at the front, by the altar, I laid down the flower.

"Thank you, God."

It was all I could say at first. And then, as my thoughts returned to the situation I was in, "Help me, God. Help me. It feels like I'm in a dark place, God. I don't want to go back to the streets. But right now I'm afraid. If I run, I'll get beaten up again. But how can I do anything else? Help me God. Help me."

I looked up. Bright sunlight. The sun shone through the high windows, reflecting the yellow flower on the white table top.

Maybe, just maybe. If God has got me this far... Maybe tomorrow *could* be different?

Chapter 1
Running Before
I Was Born

She should have known better, she really should. Cindy Wharton was the school bully. But she knew better than to mess with me. Or usually she did.

This particular time though, she had been mouthing off at me from the moment I arrived at school that morning. I said nothing. I knew my moment would come.

Cindy had beautiful long blonde hair in a ponytail. I just made it a bit shorter. The moment came in art class. The scissors were to hand, so I leaned over and … I remember looking at the hair as it fell to the floor. How it drifted down.

Then the trouble of course. More than I thought. I was expelled for that particular action. One of the few schools I had ever liked – and I'd been to a lot of schools. Different schools were part of the travelling life of a family with a dad in the army. This particular place – the army school at Munster in Germany – was a school I really enjoyed. Maybe about the only one I actually did any real work in.

Life is full of 'what ifs'. What if I had stayed there? What if I had persevered with the studies I was enjoying? What if I had continued with my swimming, adding to the junior medals I had won? What if...?

School expulsion was only the latest chapter in a growing miscellany of mishaps. Some accidental. Many deliberate. I was angry. I was moody. I wanted everything but got nothing. And if you don't play by the rules, there are consequences. Boy, are there consequences!

On the run

I was on the run before I was born. In my 16 year old mother's womb I was on my way to a life of travel and a life of struggle. My father, an Anglo-Indian in the army, had his own problems. Racial abuse was common in the 1960s. It angered him. Married in Jamaica, with me well on the way, Mum and Dad moved as and when the army asked. Aldershot, Singapore, Balsall Common, Munster, Bicester. The geography was certainly varied.

I look back with fondness on those early years. Life was hard, finances were tight. But I was loved, as were the later additions to the family, my three younger brothers. My grandparents were supportive too – although being on the move meant we saw little of them.

Dad was impulsive. One time he worked through the night to make me a birthday present of a doll's house. All made from shipping boxes. Another time, Dad and I danced through the night in the middle of a field! I think Dad had a bit to drink that night, but as a young girl there was a real thrill to being with him, dancing in the moonlight in the middle of a campsite in the Mosel Valley. Such memories are precious.

My dad called me 'Princess'. I loved the name. I dreamed of being a princess. As a young child, I would draw my knight in shining armour coming to rescue me. Taking me home to his castle.

Thinking back, I'm not sure I had a 'home' as a child. Returning from Germany to a house in Bicester, Oxfordshire, was the nearest I knew to 'coming home'. After my expulsion from day school, and after a short time at a German boarding school, I never really settled again. Gone was the desire to learn. In its place, a restlessness, maybe borne out of all those travels. Whatever the reason, there was something in me as I hit my teenage years that caused me to cry out for adventure. I didn't want to be in one place. There was a world out there. Places to go, people to meet. What was the use of a school education anyway?

Homework was replaced by boyfriends. Dad, like most dads, was very protective. I was told to be home at a certain time. Each young man to cross the threshold was vetted by Dad for suitability. Needless to say, as far as he was concerned, none of them made the grade!

Then there was Terry.

Beginnings Of A Different Life

If there was one moment in my life that, looking back, I can say was a moment of immense change, it would have to be the day I met Terry. As I stepped out with him that first evening, I had no idea of how my life was about to change.

Terry was a charmer. All the girls fancied him. So I was particularly pleased to have been the one to succeed. There was a wildness about him. He was different; he didn't seem to care about what people thought of him. Here was someone it would be worth going on an adventure with. Dad warned me, but I didn't listen. Of course not. I was a young, pretty 15 year old with the world at my feet. With short skirts and low tops, I was going to date Terry, three years my senior, whatever Dad said.

I loved those first dates. We stayed out late. Too late. Well beyond the deadlines Mum and Dad had set. But what did I care? This was life; this was real.

That summer in the mid 1970s was hot. For 15 consecutive days in June and July, temperatures reached 90°F. Ideal weather for dates with your new boyfriend. We walked everywhere. Kissed often. Went too far. Terry was dreamy. He spoke of our future, of all we were going to do in life. He would show off too – and I loved it. Climbing lampposts, leaping over streams, stealing flowers from a garden for me. This was my man and I was very definitely in love.

Our small transistor radio went everywhere with us. If we were out early, it would be the Noel Edmunds Breakfast Show on Radio 1; more likely Annie Nightingale in the late evenings. We would pretend to be Elton John and Kiki Dee and sing, 'Don't Go Breaking My Heart' as loud as we could, especially if it annoyed the passers-by.

Things got tough with Mum and Dad. I was ignoring their deadlines, staying out most of the night; forgetting my homework, playing truant from school. I shouted back, ignored them, got angry with them. In the end I was banned from seeing Terry. I was grounded.

As far as I was concerned, this was just another unreasonable hurdle to be jumped over. I sneaked out after dark, saw Terry after school, went round to his mum's house. Anything but obey

Mum and Dad.

'Stay here with me Linda.'

'What did you say?'

'You heard.'

Of course I heard. Suddenly there was this churning inside, an anticipation, an excitement. A thrill of the unknown. Sleeping with Terry. More than that, the possibility of setting up a life with him. My mouth had gone dry by the time I replied. I was frightened, but at the same time, almost dizzy with pleasure at the thought of it.

'Okay,' I said. 'Okay.'

So there I was, at the age of 15, sleeping with a man I had not long met. We stayed at Terry's mums house at first, occasionally with friends. Tina, Terry's mum, seemed to understand. I liked her a lot. She'd had a hard life, her husband running away with the wife of her own son. Nothing like that was going to happen to me and Terry. I was determined our relationship was going to work. Nothing was going to stop us. I was the princess. I had my knight in shining armour.

Police Visits

The police knocked on the door early one morning. I just had time to hide. Despite them coming into the bedroom and looking around, they didn't find me. I thought it was such a game. Exhilarating and exciting – a real adventure. Here I was at 15 with the pick of the boys, living with him, sleeping with him, hiding from the police.

Despite the excitement, by the end of the next day I was feeling guilty and made the decision to return home. I wanted to be right with Mum and Dad, but at the same time had no wish to live there anymore. Tina helped me write a letter. In it I shared as well as I was able what I was going through and asked if I could stay at Tina's. There was a note from Tina too, to say she would be happy to have me.

Mum opened the door without a word.

'Mum, I'm sorry. Please read this.'

She hit me. It was a hard slap across the face. I was sent to my room, grounded again, to await Dad's return and a talking to.

Dad was angry. 'You have a choice, Linda. Either you stay here with us, or you go. If you go, we no longer have a daughter and your three brothers no longer have a sister.'

I so loved my younger brothers. What was I to do? Why couldn't I have both? Why would my parents not accept Terry? Life was so unfair.

I left.

Back with Terry and my adopted mum, Tina, I was as happy as I could be. There was an ache inside though; a feeling that all was not well. How could Mum and Dad turn their back on me? How could they reject their only daughter? I struggled daily with the rejection. But I still had Terry. I had a roof over my head and a promising future with the man I loved.

It was new, exciting and a bit wild.

I should have known it wouldn't last.

A tired, frightened figure arrived home one evening. Very different to the Terry I usually saw. He sat down, looked over at me and with a twisted smile said:

'Linda, they've fired me.'

'What do you mean? They can't just fire someone!'

'They can when you've been caught stealing.'

It felt like I'd been hit in the stomach. This was my Terry, my perfect man. My knight. Caught stealing. The shame of it. More than that – what were we to do? How could we afford to live together?

At 15, everything is pretty black and white. I had moved from the brightness of a perfect relationship to the darkness of shame, mistrust and anger in one conversation. I thought about leaving. I should have left. It would have saved so much heartache if I had left Terry at that point. Mum and Dad would have had me back. I could have gone back to school. I could have started again. At the very least, carried on accumulating swimming medals.

But all I did was walk deeper into the darkness.

In control?

I figured I was where I wanted to be. I persuaded myself I was in control. I was with Terry.

With Terry ... and with child.

At 15 years old, I wasn't sure I wanted to be pregnant. I felt too young to be a mum. I couldn't face telling my parents. I wrote a letter and got it delivered. What would they think? They didn't reply.

My life was crashing around from crisis to crisis like a ball in a pin-ball machine. I didn't mean to get pregnant. I didn't deliberately want to upset Mum and Dad. After all, wasn't I copying what they had done themselves, running away, getting pregnant so young...?

It was hard to take it in. I was pregnant. How was I supposed to feel? Mum and Dad were ignoring me. Terry was troubled with the job loss. It wasn't quite the life I'd dreamed of when I was growing up. What happened to the romance? Where were the princess, the knight and the castle now? Where had all the adventure gone? Where was the excitement, the thrill? It had been replaced with a dull ache. An awareness that something was missing, without being sure what it was.

Maybe if I tried harder? Maybe I could make it up with Mum and Dad? Maybe things would be okay if Terry could get a new job?

Not having a job was affecting Terry big time. He became subject to bouts of anger. He began to drink. What little money we did have was spent down the pub. If I dared to challenge him, he became aggressive. I'd not seen this side of him as a naïve 15 year old. But Terry had begun to change. Gone was the bravado, the reckless extravagance of his love. The wildness was still there. The extravagance too. But directed towards the pub, not towards me. Friends and bikes were replacing evenings in with his young partner. I began to wonder about the decisions I'd made.

Terry didn't leave me much spending money. What I had, I learned to use wisely. I'd spend hours in the supermarket, comparing prices, trying to find the bargains. Fray Bentos spam. Soup. Baked beans. End of line and damaged produce. And the way Terry was treating me, that's pretty much how I felt as well; end of line and damaged.

Once I saw Mum and Dad in the supermarket. My heart was pounding. I couldn't ignore them. I shouldn't ignore them. I wheeled my trolley towards them.

'Hi.'

Dad didn't look at me. Slowly and deliberately, he steered Mum's supermarket trolley past me and into the next aisle. Not a word. Not a look. 'Dad, please. Please don't ignore me! Speak to me! PLEASE! DAD!'

Nothing.

The next time I looked up, they were walking out of the supermarket towards the car. Mum was crying. So was I.

I went down to the pub that night, joining Terry and his mates. The drink masked the pain. I ended up at the pub most nights over the next few weeks. I didn't care any more. So what if we had no money to eat? At least I was with Terry. At least we could have a good time.

I lost the baby at six months.

Pain on pain

Pain was being layered on pain. I'd lost the baby. I'd lost my dreams. I'd lost my future.

There's a verse in the Bible. It says something like 'without a vision, people perish'. That was me the day I lost the baby. It felt like I'd perished inside. Everything died, not just the unborn baby. Life had no meaning. I couldn't sleep, and on the rare occasions I did doze off, I woke with nightmares. Why was this happening? I was 16 by now and I still had my whole life to live. What had I done to deserve this? If there was a God out there, He was a cruel one.

I remembered an incident when I was growing up. We were in Singapore at the time. Mum had started going to church and took me along on occasion. We started to pray together when I went to bed. We'd kneel together and say the Lord's Prayer. They were special moments for a 7 year old girl.

One day, as we were praying, Mum fell to the floor – flat out. I was worried at first, but soon realised she was still praying, and somehow God had touched her in such a way that she had to stay on the floor. In fact, she couldn't have moved off the floor if she'd wanted to. There was a power there. I recognised it, even as a child.

But now... What now? Where was God now? What could He want with me anyway? A drunk. A runaway. A rebel. Pain engulfed me. The loss of the baby crippled me mentally.

Terry was kind. At least at first. He stayed in a while. And when he did start going back to the pub, I went with him. I didn't like to admit it, but I was out of control. Alcohol was taking over.

Patterns

It was a beautiful summer evening. Terry and I had stayed late at the pub. We weren't totally drunk, but were not exactly walking in a straight line as we made our way home. As we passed one of the houses, we noticed the garage door was open. I reasoned to myself it was their fault. If you don't close your garage doors at night, what do you expect? Here we were, a bit drunk – and very broke. We had no food at home. But we had to eat.

I wonder whether the owners ever missed that joint of beef? Did they ever notice? We left the deep freeze looking exactly as it was, covering up the space where the meat had been with a few frozen fruit pies. We laughed that night. More than we had for a long time. It was almost a relief to both of us to be doing something together. Something we shared, that no one else could possibly know. We went to bed late. And on full stomachs. I woke up frightened. What had we done the night before? It seemed like we had stepped over a line.

'Come on, darling. It doesn't matter. We need it.'

It was the next evening when Terry asked me to steal again. I refused. His reaction was almost violent. Almost. I was frightened of stealing again. And maybe, just maybe, I was frightened of

Terry as well. But for now, I wouldn't do it.

It didn't stop Terry. That night, there was more meat on the table. And the night after. Once you have stolen, the second time is easier. You rationalise it, pretend it's for a good reason. Pretend you are a 'Robin Hood' type figure, stealing from the rich.

Sometimes, the garage doors weren't open, but it was easy to break in. No one saw him.

It became a habit. Patterns were beginning to form. Drinks at the pub. I went home first. Terry would wait until it was late. Go a different way home each night. Try and find an open garage. If not, break in. Most of them had deep freezers. And the ones that didn't? It wasn't too hard to find buyers for garden equipment.

Getting Married

I was 17 years old and 7 months pregnant with Georgie by the time Terry and I got married. Like the rest of my new life, it was a rushed, tired and unromantic day. We figured we should marry for the sake of the child. So it was down to the local registry office with a few friends and a bit of a buffet meal afterwards.

My parents came reluctantly. They spent most of the evening before trying to get me drunk and admit that I didn't want to marry Terry. I think they were right, but it was no use trying to change my mind. I was headstrong, intent on doing things my way. No way were they going to stop me. But even as I ignored their pleas, I knew I was doing the wrong thing. I was being driven by my own stubbornness, my own recklessness. I was desperately ignoring the facts.

I loved Terry, or thought I did. But we were drunk a lot of the time now. We were broke all of the time. We were petty thieves.

We were unstable. The ball on the pinball machine seemed to be moving faster, hitting more things. I felt even more out of control.

The romance and adventure had vanished and the dull ache persisted. I was still trying harder. Still hoping I could make it up with Mum and Dad. Still hoping Terry could get a new job. Maybe if we could get a council home instead of staying with Terry's mum? But there it was – a week after a short honeymoon, we were down the pub again. Drinking, stealing, living hand to mouth. What kind of a world was I bringing our baby into?

Now and again I prayed. I asked for God's help. I'm sure many of us do that. At points of crisis. At points of desperation. I had no idea that God had designs on my life. No idea that He loved me no matter what. No idea that He wanted me to know Him, to allow Him to change my life. Those moments on the bedroom floor in Singapore seemed a lifetime ago.

Arrest

It was about 9.30am on a Tuesday morning when they called. The sun was shining. The tulips had just come into bloom in the garden. The two policemen looked very smart in their uniforms. Peaked caps rather than helmets. And a police car at the end of the drive.

'Good morning, madam. I wonder whether we could have a quick word with you?'

'Of course. Come in. What's the matter? What's happened?'

'I wonder whether you would mind telling us where your husband was last night?'

I held my breath, bit my lip. I didn't want to say anything in case it got Terry into more trouble than he was obviously already in.

'I gather he wasn't at home?'

I shook my head.

'Your husband has been caught in a robbery. He resisted arrest. He's charged with theft and GBH.'

Numbness. I couldn't feel a thing. I stared at the wall, concentrating on a small tear in the wallpaper. I'd never noticed it before. Must get it fixed sometime. A bit of glue would do it. 'Are you alright? Did you hear what we said?'

'Yes, I heard.'

Thankfully, Terry was only put on remand for that one. But I was scared. Georgie was due to arrive at any moment and here I was, with the possibility of being on my own. A husband with a criminal record. Parents not talking to me. No money. No future. Where was that princess now?

Chapter 2
Left For Dead

Dreams are strange things. It seems to me there are two types. Those you want. And those you don't.

My dreams had changed. Now in our own council house, I would wake in the night, frightened and alone. Even when Terry was there, I still felt alone. My husband had abandoned me in favour of drinking and motorbikes. My parents had abandoned me to my own choices. God had abandoned me too, or so it seemed to me. What use is a God when He doesn't answer your prayers for food on the table?

And if it wasn't nightmares, it was Georgie. A parent at 17, it wasn't easy for me, especially as Terry was not there most of the time and when he was, he would refuse to help.

It was asking for help that nearly killed me.

But I must go back in time a while. Those first days after Georgie's birth were wonderful. I was a proud mum. Terry, by then on bail for beating up his step-father, was home with me. He was proud of me. I was proud of me! Little Georgie brought some peace as well between me and Mum and Dad. The healing touch of a baby's hand.

Of course, it didn't last. The peace and pleasure brought about by Georgie was shattered a few days later.

'Put her down!'

'I can't! She's crying.'

A push. I fell onto the sofa, guarding Georgie's head as I fell.

'Stop it Terry, you'll hurt her.'

'She's not my child anyway.'

'What?'

'You heard what I said.'

'How dare you! She can only be yours.'

Terry walked away, maybe shamed by what he'd said.

It was soon after that I decided I didn't want to live in our own house when Terry was inside. It would be much better to stay with Tina, Terry's mum. It became a pattern. Living with Tina when Terry was in prison, so there would be no accusations of another man. Then back to our own council house when Terry was released. Tina being around during that time was one of the few blessings. She was able to help in keeping Terry under control.

Keeping my husband under control.

Is that what it had come to?

There was no controlling him, of course. He was back at the pub as soon as he was out of prison. He'd be away for most of the week, regularly with other women. That's what hurt the most. I felt so ashamed that he needed another woman to satisfy him. At the same time, so angry that he would accuse me of being unfaithful, when it was him all the time, and right in front of me, with no attempt at concealment.

My friends told me I was a fool to stay with him.

I was.

Some days, I would go for long walks with Georgie in the pram. I loved those walks. The long journey over to Garth Park. Then sitting on a bench, smoking, thinking, dreaming. Georgie was a complete delight. She attracted attention too, of course. I got to know some of the mums. I could manage a whole day like that, especially if the weather was kind. My troubles were like my house, miles away. Another life away. The only problem was having to walk back into that life. The walk home was always slower than the walk over to the park.

Terry wasn't around a lot of the time, but I could guarantee he would always be there on a Monday. That was the day I got my social security money. He used to leave me enough for food and take the rest. Our ideas of 'enough' were not the same. It was hard to manage. The Co-op was just down the street. I never got caught. Shoplifting became another habit alongside the excessive drinking.

And not just drinking. By now I was on prescription drugs for depression – the strongest dose allowed. When Tina was out and Georgie asleep, I would spend hours on the sofa, just staring out of the window, counting the flowers in the garden, high on my prescription valium.

My Fault

I didn't feel a thing. Really, I didn't. When he first hit me, I was so shocked, there simply wasn't any pain. I reasoned that I deserved it. It was my fault. I'd been swearing at him, shouting that he was useless, a hopeless husband. I had pushed him too far. I reasoned he was within his rights to hit me. The main bruising was on my shoulder. I could keep it hidden. A bit of swelling above the lip; nothing make-up couldn't fix.

The next morning, I wasn't so sure. Surely he shouldn't hit his wife? What was normal? To be honest, I didn't know. I hadn't ever seen Dad hit my mum – though there had been some pretty big shouting matches. I decided to say nothing and do nothing. Terry came home early from the pub the next night. A bit the worse for wear with drink, but so sorry for what he had done. He was almost in tears. We hugged. I said I loved him. He said he would never do it again.

Next time it was harder to cover up. I had a massive lump above my eye where he had hit me with his fist. I had to pretend to my friends that I had fallen and hit my head against a door. Silly Linda. So clumsy. I think they believed me.

I was becoming frightened of my own husband. What mood would he be in when he came back from the pub? How drunk would he be? Maybe if I went to bed early and pretended to be asleep, he would leave me alone? Sometimes it worked.

I knew something was desperately wrong. I no longer trusted Terry. I was fearful of him, wondering how long it would be before he became violent again. I soon found out.

Terry became more moody, more depressed. And the more depressed he was, the more violent he became. This time it was not just me I had to protect. What if he hurt Georgie? Maybe I should run away? The thought gnawed at me – run away, be rid of him. But where to? Who would look after me? Mum and Dad were still disowning me, my brothers were still young and Dad was about to be posted to Dusseldorf anyway. Who else could there be? No one. I locked the idea away; threw away the key.

I lived in fear of my life. Tina was working nights. No one

calling round to hear the screams. Every day was clouded with the thought that Terry would come home drunk and beat me up. Even if he didn't, the fear was still there. I lost weight, I looked frightened. I was frightened.

Terry began to play mind games with me. He knew I was afraid. He would play on it, suggesting he would hit me, then saying he loved me. Hugging me one moment, then in the next breath winding me in the stomach and pushing me across the room. He would ask me questions. Stupid questions. If I said the right answer, I escaped being hurt. If not...

It was complete control. Emotional manipulation I guess you'd call it. Every moment of the day, I found myself thinking about Terry. What mood he would be in. Trying to please him. Doing anything to win his approval. He completely owned me. I was caught up within his moods, his pleasures, fearing his fists. I find it hard to look back at that time. My mind has blocked out some of the memories. Nor was I thinking straight. I was high on valium a lot of the time. When I tried to get off the tablets it felt like I was on the verge of a breakdown. I wanted to leave, but was too frightened to do so. Maybe if we had another child, all would be well. Matt arrived two years after his sister.

Prison and Pubs

I really should have known that a second child would not improve things. Once again, Terry was in and out of prison. He was allowed out for a week or two after Matt was born. After finally being released for good, he was soon spending all his time and money at the pub again. And sadly, he was with other women a lot of the time. With Tina's support, I threw him out of the house. But that wasn't to last either. He'd come back tearful and seemingly penitent. And like a fool, I would believe him.

'Linda! Linda! Have you heard what's happened to Terry?!'

I was sure the message from my friend Anna was not going to be good news. Terry had been arrested again. It took ten policemen to contain his rage. Prison was the result. Again.

My feelings were mixed. It was a relief, but at the same time, I had no love for the police and am sure that had I been there, I'd have been fighting too. I already had a record for resisting arrest from one of our earlier skirmishes.

One morning as I was seeing to Matt there was a voice at the bedroom door. 'Hi darlin, pleased to see me?' A short sentence from Terry that changed everything again. And a shorter sentence in prison this time, meaning he was back.

But with Terry free, it was me that was feeling locked up. Abuse was common now. I was forever wearing heavy make-up to deal with the bruises. People have asked me why I never went to the authorities. But for me, the authorities – especially the police – were the enemy. They were the ones that had it in for my husband. I was still the loyal wife, still wanting the marriage to work, still hoping Terry would change once he found work. The only work he ever found, though, was of the criminal variety. To be fair, it was hard for Terry to find work. Ours was a comparatively small community. Everyone knew of Terry's prison sentences and his violence. No one would take him on. I worked instead, in an Oxfam warehouse. Tina would look after the children while I worked and I would walk 3 miles each day to Tina's to drop off the children and a further mile to work. The same again in reverse at the end of the day. No wonder I was always tired.

The day we celebrated my friend Anna's birthday was

beautiful. Right through to the warm evening we stayed down the pub with friends and drank. Finally, it was time to go home. Tina was looking after the kids and Terry might be around there too. I'd had too much to drink so was grateful for John offering his scooter to sit on as he pushed it along. 'Come on,' said Anna, 'put the helmet on too. You're so pissed you're going to roll off it!' Thank you, Anna, for saving my life that night.

Terry saw us coming. There was anger in his eyes, swear words in his mouth. 'What do you think you are doing?! Where have you been? Get off that bike. Get home now!' As he reached me, he took hold of me, lifting me into the air. John and Anna tried to stop him. Both were pushed to the ground.

Then it happened.

With all his considerable strength, he threw me. I fell and my head smashed against the curb. Extensive injuries to my knee and shoulder. And a dent in the scooter helmet that saved me from certain death.

The police arrived and an ambulance. 'Come on, Linda, we know he threw you. Make a complaint,' said the police woman. I stayed silent.

Sergeant Boyle from the CID was harder work a few days later. 'Linda, we know what's happening. Just tell us. We can press charges. We can put him away for what he's doing to you. Tell us what happened.'

'I fell down the stairs.'

Safety

Anna and my friends didn't stop trying to persuade me to turn Terry in for the violence against me that, by now, was nearly a daily occurrence. Part of me wanted to go to the police, but part of me still felt that somehow it was my fault. It was my punishment for being such a hapless wife and mother. Plus there were the continued threats from Terry to help keep me quiet. 'If you say anything to the police or social services, I'll kill you.' Terry was pretty direct with his words.

It got to the stage where I had to do something. I was imprisoned at home, fearful to go out with friends, afraid to leave the children in Terry's care. Even Tina was encouraging me to escape. Terry's brother Phil came to stay for a while. It wasn't long before he too was adding his voice to those encouraging me to leave.

With a heavy heart, on a Sunday evening, I said my farewells to Tina, wrapped the children up and headed for Oxford and a refuge for battered women. I cried nearly all the way there. What kind of mother took her children away in the night?

One that wanted to live.

I found kindness, understanding and rest. But not for long. Two weeks into my stay there was a banging on the front door. Incessant banging. Shouting too. I knew the voice. 'Linda! Linda! Come home! I need you! I'm sorry, please come home!'

Like a fool I believed him when he said he'd changed. I looked at my children. They needed a father. I went home with Terry.

I remember praying.

Every time I saw Georgie and Matt, there was a prayer on my lips. Prayers for their protection mostly. But for me too. That time in Singapore with my mum came back to me again. God had been there. God knew about me. God cared. Fleetingly, I believed again. Prayers to a God who loved me. Prayers to a God who could help me.

Asking for help. But no sooner prayed than forgotten.

Left for dead

I said at the start of the chapter that it was asking for help that nearly killed me. This is how it happened.

Sunday evening was ironing time. It was a regular event, preparing enough clothes for the week ahead. Terry was home and seemed to be in a good mood. 'Darling,' I said, 'be a good boy and get me a cup of tea would you, while I finish this?'

A push. I was on the floor.

'Don't you EVER ask me to be your slave!'

'I wasn't. I didn't mean anything by it.'

I saw the iron coming and just ducked in time. If the table still exists, you'll see there's a chunk of wood out of it to this day. I wasn't quick enough to run. Terry was swearing and shaking me like a rag doll. Then he was banging my head on the floor. I was screaming and just able to stay conscious. More kicking, more fists. I remember one to the side of my face as I passed out.

I came round to find Terry filling my mouth with valium tablets. 'Swallow them you bitch. Swallow!' I kept my mouth firmly shut. Until he held my nose. As I opened my mouth, he forced more tablets in, making me swallow by holding my throat. All the time banging my head against the floor. I passed out again.

Chapter 3
"Mummy, Come Home."

I'm so grateful to Jeanette.

My neighbour had her own problems with men, but nothing like dealing with Terry. She had listened to the shouting and the banging. Somehow she knew it was more serious than just some kind of marital slanging match. She saw Terry running from the house. Within a minute, she was through the back door and trying to bring me round.

I got to the hospital in time. They pumped my stomach and insisted I stayed there. More police interviews. More silence from me. What a fool I was not to say something.

Staring at the hospital ceiling, I knew I was lucky to still be alive. But with that thought came a feeling of hopelessness. What was I to do? I wouldn't speak to the police. Nor to the hospital chaplain who came to see me. My mind was reliving the episode. Over and over. I couldn't sleep. In the end I took the sleeping tablets I was offered.

Back home and back to work. It was when I dropped the

children off that I saw Tina's look of concern. 'You can't do this. You can't pretend this just didn't happen! You have to go. You're going to end up six feet under. Terry will be in jail for murder. For the sake of your life and your sanity, just go. I'll look after the kids. Come back when you want. But go. Go now. Before Terry comes back.'

She was right of course. As I stood on Tina's doorstep, I plucked up the courage. It was a big decision, especially leaving Georgie and little Matt. I went back home, packed a few clothes and found I had enough money to get me as far as London. Surely there would be a job for me there? I could work hard, get myself a place, bring the kids down when it was safe to do so.

Cold and Hungry

It was a bit nerve-racking walking into the Thistle Hotel and asking to see the staff manager. The lady was very polite, almost concerned for me, but couldn't offer me a job. Never mind, I thought, there's plenty of other hotels. All I need is to swing the job and they would give me a bed as well, wouldn't they? And so the day went. Hotel after hotel. Then, when that didn't seem to be working, store after store, shop after shop.

It felt like I walked everywhere on that first day in London. Called in at pretty much every hotel and shop I came to. I smiled, said the right things, offered to work for whatever they could pay. And got nowhere. When evening came, I was cold and hungry. With no real idea of what to do or where to go.

It was November. A whole day on my feet and wearing insufficient clothing. I felt so tired. And very cold. The tears came. I told myself off, not to be so silly. It was just the first day, what did I expect?

I tried sleeping in a park, but that was foolish. By midnight, the cold was so great, I was beginning to lose feeling in my hands and feet. I walked for a while, found a warm air vent next to a shop, dozed for an hour or two. Spent some of the little money I had on an early morning coffee to warm up.

I began to wonder whether I was really going to get work by about day three. I had called at just about every hotel and store I could think of. No work. No one wanted an unskilled cleaner or shop assistant. I tried to make myself look good, but sleeping rough meant that it was pretty evident I was not the kind of employee they wanted.

Stuart was from Glasgow. He had been on the streets for years. It was kind of him to share his bottle of whisky with me. Kinder still to show me how to sleep out and keep myself warm. The alcohol seemed to help. I started drinking just to stay warm. It helped with the long night hours. Lulled me to sleep in the end.

'A lass like you shouldn't be on the streets, love.'

'But what can I do, Stuart? I can't go home.'

'Here, let me take you...'

Stuart introduced me to Brenda at Centrepoint, a hostel in London that was specifically there for homeless young people. Brenda was so kind. She listened. She helped me clean myself up. Helped me get on the job trail again. And she prayed with me. Somehow she sensed that I knew there was a God and that He was there to help me if only I would ask. I found great comfort in those prayers and such support from the Centre. Just to have a warm bed and a shower was beyond my greatest hopes at that time.

How quickly I had grown used to the streets.

Cardboard City

The only problem with Centrepoint was that they were strict about drink. I had been in London for a few weeks now and had quickly got used to the drinking. It reminded me of the days in the pub at home. It helped me keep warm, sleep, and most of all, it masked the gnawing emptiness inside. I was crying out for real life and love. For people who cared. And most of all for my children. A bottle of vodka was a poor substitute.

Most nights I was too drunk to go to Centrepoint, so I ended up with Stuart and others in Cardboard City. Just under the bridge at Charing Cross was a vast array of home-made beds. Cardboard flooring, sleeping bags donated by local charities, and then more cardboard and newspaper on top to help keep the cold out. Sometimes we made a fire as well, although the police weren't too keen on that.

Cardboard City was a comparatively safe place. My fellow drunks were protective of me and helpful in ensuring I got something to eat from the kind people that came by with food. But out in the streets, out in London, it was a different matter.

Hyde Park is a big area. I thought it would be safe enough to walk through, but there are not many people there late at night, and little in the way of lighting. I noticed too late the big guy behind me.

He was about thirty feet back but walking briskly and in my direction. I thought I was being silly at first, that he would just pass me by. It was just a coincidence that he was there.

To make sure, I turned down a path to the left. He followed. I looked back. Maybe twenty feet away now. He smiled. I saw his white teeth through the gloom.

'Hello darling,' he shouted. 'What's your name then?'

I ran. He ran faster. The adrenaline was pumping. If I could get back around and onto the main path, I'd be safer. Less bushes around, nowhere he could drag me. My shoes were slowing me down. High heels. I kicked them off. Ran faster still. I could see a light in the distance. Headed towards it. But not fast enough.

The whole scene seemed to be in slow motion. I could hear his breathing now. He was calling me to stop. Said he just wanted to talk. Almost beside me. Grabbing at my cardigan. I struggled to free myself, hitting out for all I was worth, pummelling his body. I was thrown to the floor.

'No! Stop! Help! Somebody help me!'

His hands were all over me. Too big and powerful to throw off. He pinned me down with his legs, his hands pushing my shoulders to the ground. I screamed. He put his hand over my mouth.

I struggled for a while, but it hurts less if you just stay still.

A few minutes later he was gone. I dragged my jeans back up and began to look for my shoes. I was physically shaking, shuddering. Just couldn't stop. Then I was sick.

I know. I should have gone to the police. But I still had this irrational hate of them. And who was going to listen to a 19 year old girl on the streets when she claimed she had been raped? I was a missing person officially, and that too may have caused problems I wasn't willing to face.

That night I drank meths. It was a quicker fix. Anything to forget. The children. Terry. The abuse. The rape.

Curled up in my sleeping bag, the tears came. Soft tears. Quietly falling. More and more of them, wetting the cardboard beneath me. I felt so alone. No one knew what had happened. No one cared. Maybe it was time to go. Go for good I mean. In front of a train maybe. Or jump into the Thames.

I shuddered again. No. I can't do that. There must be a way out. Then the prayers came. 'God! Please God! Help me! If you're there, please do something. I'm lost. So, so lost.'

Through the pain and the alcohol, I felt Him. I knew He was there. The God of my childhood. The Bible talks about a 'peace that passes understanding'. That's exactly how it was ... I couldn't begin to understand how it was that I'd got here, this low, this hurt, dampening the cardboard with my tears. But I knew for a moment in my pain, the gentle hand of an invisible God. Despite the shock, I slept better that night than I had for a long time.

The Sunday Mirror

It was a Sunday morning. I'd stayed sober the night before, which got me a bed at Centrepoint.

'Linda! Linda, look!' Brenda wasn't the sort of lady to get excited. From a middle class background, well dressed, a bit prim and proper really. So, for her to be shouting at the top of her voice meant something big.

'Look. It's in the Sunday Mirror! It's you! The children!'

There, staring at me was a headline: 'Mummy, Come Home'. My photo was there. And so were the children's. I broke. Convulsed with deep, deep sobs. There were my two children looking at me. I had left them. Abandoned them.

But the real sadness was to be found in the news story that followed. Tina was dead. She'd died within a few short weeks from an aggressive form of cancer. Friends were helping with the children, but I had to go. How could I stay in London, whatever the danger to me from Terry, when Georgie and Matt needed me? Brenda helped me speak with the probation service and get a promise from Terry not to harm me. She gave me the train fare. I was on my way.

No Change

Back at the house, Terry seemed a lot quieter and reflective. Sad about his mum, of course, but maybe more than that. I began to hope.

I tried to get back into the old routines. Walks to the park. Taking Matt on the swings. Tuesday evenings at the social club, watching Georgie charm everyone with her dancing moves. Back home, I would turn the record player up loud, drown out the world with the latest soul albums. The O'Jay's, Rose Royce, Diana Ross. Singing Chaka Kahn's 'I'm Every Woman' at the top of my voice.

'I'm every woman, it's all in me. Anything you want done, baby, I'll do it naturally.'

The truth is, I wasn't every woman. I was different. I was a punch bag. I was depressed. I was desperate. There was nothing natural left in me. Nothing left in our marriage – other than pain.

The strange thing about those first days back was the total lack of communication about where I had been and what I had been doing. It was as if I hadn't been away. Terry accepted me around the house as if I had been there every moment. I had my stories planned. What I was going to say. What I wouldn't share with him. But in the end, he just didn't ask. It became a bit unnerving after a while. The pressure began to show. I wasn't sure how to take him. Was this for real or was he playing mind games again? It wasn't long before I was back on the valium.

Terry still didn't have a job. After Tina's funeral, it was back to the pub. Back to other girls too. I played my old game, pretending to sleep when he came home. It worked most of the time.

One night he came home and started banging his head against the bedroom wall. I could see him through my partially closed eyes. Harder and harder. I wanted to shout at him to stop, but knew that if I did, he may well turn on me. Terry's brother Phil was staying, following the funeral. We spoke the next day about it.

'I don't know, Linda. I think something's very wrong with him. This isn't just depression, it's madness! Please be careful.'

On the Road Again

It was a Sunday afternoon. Terry had been watching some sort of football results programme. Manchester United had beaten Crystal Palace 2-0. Funny how you remember the strangest things at a point of crisis. The children were out at a birthday party. Terry had started to peel potatoes for me, using his beloved Bowie knife. In fact, Terry had a thing for knives. Quite a collection. But the Bowie was his favourite.

I really don't know if there was a reason. I don't remember us having an argument. I don't remember upsetting him. I was very careful not to.

I had been taking advantage of the children's absence to do some cleaning and was polishing the sideboard. Suddenly, the knife was in the door frame a couple of inches away from where my shoulder had been. I turned around, but too late to run. He grabbed me, threw me to the ground and started kicking me. I managed to get to my knees, but not quick enough to get away. He had his hands around my throat and started to bang my head against the floor. I was screaming. My nose felt like it was broken. There was a lot of blood.

Phil came into the room just in time and pushed Terry away

from me. Fists were flying. Phil managed to wrestle Terry to the floor. Terry was out of control, screaming, swearing, shouting, kicking. Phil looked up at me and shouted.

'Linda, run! For God's sake, run!'

I didn't need a second invitation.

I was out of the door and running as fast as I could, taking a short cut over a field to the main road. I flagged a couple down in their car. I must have looked quite a sight, blood pouring from my nose. They were very kind and even gave me the coach fare to get back to London.

The next time I would see Terry, he'd be on his death bed.

Chapter 4
"Just 10 Minutes, Love."

Victoria Coach Station is remarkably busy late at night. As I walked down the concourse, there were hundreds of people around, pushing past me, in a hurry to be on their way. People to see. Places to go. But I was in no sort of rush.

Still in a daze, I stared into the bright lights. I wanted to cower in the corners, get out of the light, away from people. Just to curl up on my own in a safe place. Where to go? What to do?

I had stemmed the bleeding and wrapped my cardigan tightly around me. Partly to stop anyone seeing the blood on my blouse, partly to keep warm. I walked through the terminal one slow step at a time, out into the night air. What now? I had enough for a coffee. A good place to start.

I took my time, made the coffee last nearly an hour and a half. I was in shock, not sure what to do, where to go. Phil and his family would take care of the children. But what about me? I was the child at that moment. Where should I go?

Lenny had invited me to stay before. He ran a strip club in

Soho and I'd been careful to stay clear. But at that moment, in the café near Victoria, I made another of those life-changing decisions. I had no warm clothes, my blouse was blood-stained and when the coffee ran out, I had to move on.

It was morning by the time I passed by Buckingham Palace. The flag was flying. I think that means she's at home. I wondered whether she was still asleep. I guessed someone brought her breakfast in bed. I thought I'd be a princess at one time. Now look at me.

'Hello love. Good grief, what's happened to you? Come in.' Lenny lived next to the strip club on Greek Street. He listened carefully, gave me a change of clothes, even if they were a men's t-shirt and shorts!

'Stay here. You must. Take a few days out. Take your time. You poor thing.'

I liked him. His kindness was genuine, I think. The spare bed was made up and I had a home. Or, at least, a temporary one. Time to think. Time to catch my breath.

Just 10 Minutes, Love

'Don't go back living rough again, Linda. You'll only get messed up again. Stay here. You'll need to work, of course, but it's just ten minutes, love. That's all. Just ten minutes an hour. Good pay too.'

Lenny had his hand on my shoulder, concern in his face. He wasn't forcing me, but I needed to stay somewhere. And yes, it was just ten minutes an hour in the strip club. Up on a stage. No touching. And, after all, I had a good body. Why not use it?

That was the logic. Lenny had approached me before during my earlier London stay, but I'd had the sense to walk away. Not now though. Like a fly in his spider's web, he'd caught me and was reeling me in. I felt trapped, unable to pull away. But I felt flattered too. There were lots of compliments about my body. And it had been a long time since I had heard any compliments. And here, seemingly, was a gentleman who cared. Hitting someone was just not in his world. He was in his forties, but still good looking, dark and brooding, reflecting his Maltese heritage. He'd bought me some clothes by this time too. He didn't have to do that, I reasoned. He must mean well.

I took a long walk through the streets, arguing with myself. I was repulsed at the thought of taking my clothes off for some perverted old men in a strip club. But it was the most secure I had felt in months. I had a roof over my head and the prospect of having my own money. I'd never had my own money. Terry only left me a few pennies to live on. I'd not bought any clothes in years. I stopped at a dress shop. They looked so nice. To be able to walk in and buy something!

And as Lenny said, it was only ten minutes.

Dressed in a sequined low cut dress, I stood at the side of the small stage. The music started. I looked up into the lights, again crying out for the shadows, anywhere but here. Anywhere to hide. But there was nowhere to go. Nothing to do but to just get on with it. Forcing a smile, controlling my nerves, I walked on to the stage.

I cried, of course. The first time. And the second. But you became numb after a while. Some men gave you tips – quite generous on occasion. You learned to deal with the perverts. Lenny was a good minder. And the money was coming in.

In the end it was ten minutes three times an hour. I signed up with a couple of other strip clubs in the same area and went between them. Linda the professional. But what a profession.

Security

I didn't love Lenny. I never did love him. But I was flattered by his attentions. He took special care of his number one strip club girl. It wasn't long before I moved over to his bed.

I think it would be easy for people to judge me for the decisions I took, but this was the first secure place I had found in years. Actually, pretty much the first security I had ever known. No moving between army bases with my parents. No threats of violence from Terry. I was off prescription drugs and my drinking was moderate. And if I could just let go of the nagging guilt of my children for a while, this was a good time for me.

I argued that as soon as I had made enough money, I would quit the strip club, find a flat and bring the children down. I hadn't made enough money by the time the Salvation Army knocked on the door.

Four Days to Live

'Miss Linda Smith?' I used an alias, not so much for the work at the strip club as to not be found by Terry. But the Salvation Army knew who I was. I still don't know how they found me – I forgot to ask. Maybe it was Stuart and his friends in Cardboard City. I nodded to the Salvation Army officer. She smiled and asked to come in.

Each with a mug of tea, we sat in the kitchen.

'I'm so sorry to have to bring you bad news,' she said. 'The police have been trying to trace you and asked us to help. It's your mother. She's very ill and wants to see you.'

Silence. I heard a car pass outside. It felt unreal. As if I was in another world from the sounds around me. Blinking back the tears, I struggled to put the mug down without dropping it. 'I'm sorry? What did you say?'

It was cancer. By the time I got up to my parents' new home in Holbeach near Peterborough, Mum looked so frail. An old woman at 37 years. She was frightened to sleep in case she died. Dad said she had been given only four days to live.

I spent every moment I could with Mum. My younger brothers were there too.

I did my apologising, of course. 'Mum, Dad, I'm so sorry to be such a disappointment to you.' I lied about what I was doing in London. Of course I did. Made out that I had a secretarial job. They weren't to know I couldn't type. And they were never to know what I actually did.

Dad encouraged me to get some sleep, to leave Mum alone and to remember her how she used to be. He was pretty insistent, but I refused to leave Mum's side.

'Dad, you may want to be miserable on your own, but I'm staying with Mum – she needs me.'

I bought Mum the biggest bunch of flowers I could afford. Anything to brighten the room. We talked a lot, about the past. Her meeting Dad. Me being born. Singapore too; the time when Mum was so powerfully impacted by what seemed to be God's very presence in the room. Mum had retained her faith in God and it came to the fore now. I was challenged by it. Despite all she had been through, she believed in God. It seemed to sustain her. And as the fourth day passed, she was still with us. And the fifth. And the sixth. Amazingly she seemed stronger.

If this was God at work, I wanted to know more. That Sunday, I went to Fleet Parish Church of Mary Magdalene, near Holbeach.

It's a big medieval thing. Full of pews and musty smells. Is this where I'd find God? I wasn't sure about that. But I attended the boring service, I listened to the boring sermon and I prayed. I prayed like I hadn't ever prayed.

'God, if you're there, please either heal Mum or take her. I hate to see her so weak, so old. Take her or heal her Lord.'

He took her.

Same Day, Same Time

Mum lived two months, not four days, but in the end the cancer caught up with her.

In a way, though, I saw Mum defeat the cancer. The frailer she looked, the stronger her Christian faith became. She seemed ready to go. Near the end, with a failing voice, I heard her pray. She recited the Lord's Prayer out loud. I was the only one in the room. I joined in. By the time we got to 'Yours is the power and the glory,' Mum's voice was stronger and we were both in tears. I couldn't stop crying that day. It looked like I was losing Mum at a young age, but at the same time, I saw someone ready to go, at peace with God, confident in her simple faith.

The Lord's Prayer became part of my life from that day. I often recited it, remembering the prayer at Mum's bedside. 'Lord, give me this day my daily bread...' That was the part I prayed most.

Mum died at 3.30pm on 1st August, aged 37. I helped to tidy up the house, sort out some of her possessions and found her christening certificate. She was baptised at 3.30pm on 1st August 37 years earlier. The same day. The same time. I took it as a sign. Even in our darkest of times, somehow God knew what He was doing.

The same day. The same time. What were the chances? It was

too much of a coincidence. I wasn't sure what to make of it, but the thought that God had somehow been there as my Mum died stayed with me.

The problem was I was back in the same job. The same day. The same time. The same ten minutes. Thoughts of God faded as my 'just ten minutes' became the pattern of the day, the days and the months that followed.

I didn't love Lenny, but he was good to me. I stayed with him. My income began to increase. Maybe, just maybe, I could get out of this job and bring the children to London?

Two Phone Calls

It was later the next year that I heard Dad wasn't too well, so a rare thing for me – I phoned him. He'd been having headaches, which he had put down to paint fumes from repainting the house. But it wasn't that. The hospital identified a cyst on the brain.

'But it's nothing that radiotherapy can't fix, Princess. I'll be fine.'

We talked a long while. We laughed, talked of Mum, of me taking a break and meeting up with him.

The next week, Dad called me. He was excited. The radiotherapy was to start on Tuesday. He was going to be fine. Another long talk with him. Making up for lost time really. Finally, we said our goodbye's.

'Goodnight Princess. Take care. I love you.'

They were the last words I ever heard him say. The very next day my brother Paul called. He was in tears. Dad had died in the night. The growth was more advanced than anyone had thought.

He died on Remembrance Sunday. Even today, I always

remember to buy a poppy.

I put the phone down in disbelief. How could this happen? Both my parents in just over a year. Both still in their thirties.

It was too much for me to take in. I screamed, shouted, swore; ripped the phone from the wall and threw it across the room. I smashed the vase, the picture, the television set. Still in my dressing gown I ran down the street, screaming at the top of my voice, out of control, out of my mind. Lenny called the medics, I was sedated.

Angry. Confused. Beyond comfort. They were dark days. Dad died just over a year after Mum. I was back in London after the funeral. There was no God after all. How could any God be so cruel? I found my god in the vodka bottle.

I was so aware I needed a new beginning. Just not the one that was offered to me.

Chapter 5
Modern Slavery

'Linda, you need a change.'

'I know. But what Lenny?'

'I've got an idea. I'm opening a new strip club in Southampton. I'd like you to be my headline act.'

It wasn't exactly the kind of new start I was hoping for. But I was flattered. Lenny continued to care for me. He saw my need for change and, in his own limited way, was offering a way out of the crisis I was in. If I stayed in London, it was likely I'd end up drinking again, just to forget the past; Mum and Dad, the children. I said 'yes'.

The first few weeks were quite exciting. A new venture, sharing the challenge of opening the club with Lenny. It was strange though. I felt I was doing well with the stage routines, but Lenny was restless. It all came out in a conversation one morning.

'Linda, will you go on the streets for me?'

'What?!'

'On the streets. There's a lot more money out there. I'll make sure you are well paid.'

'Lenny, are you asking me to be a prostitute?!'

'You'd still be my girl, Linda. I'd look after you.'

I had no idea that Lenny was already running girls on the streets of Southampton and that he'd been doing so for some time, well before he opened the strip club. Had he been fooling me all along? Had there always been another motive? I felt cheated, let down. Here was someone who had seemed to care for me, but I guess in the end the love of money had won over and above any affection for me. I was being used again.

Moving On

Sheridan had called around a few times. At six foot three, he was an attractive black man, clearly worked out in the gym and had a big, ready smile. I had flirted with him. He'd been in to see my show, bought me a drink or two as well. Sheridan had heard of my conversation with Lenny.

'Come and live with me, Linda. You don't have to live like this, I'll look after you.'

I was desperate. And naïve.

Within a week of that conversation I had left Lenny, given up the strip club and moved in with Sheridan. He sold cars for a living and was good at it too. When he wasn't doing that, he worked as a DJ in the bars and clubs. Here was someone who had a legitimate job. I could find a job too. We'd be a real couple with real jobs!

I had always smoked a bit, but Sheridan was smoking something completely different. I liked it. Our first summer in Southampton was a glorious blur... Late evenings in the garden, lying down, staring at the sky as the stars came out, not really sure what time it was, or even where I was. Cannabis became part of my daily life. We gave it many names: weed, hash, dope ... escape.

One of the problems with smoking dope is that it dulls your senses. You don't think straight. You don't notice things. I never asked Sheridan where he was going most evenings. I didn't notice anything strange with the many conversations he had with girls out on the streets. I didn't notice the white powder packages he was receiving and passing on.

One evening we went for a meal with Garth and Erica. They lived in a third storey flat just across the road from us and had become good friends. Erica was on the streets, I knew that. Part way through the evening, Sheridan and Garth went out for a smoke. That's when Erica began to talk about her life on the streets. It was fascinating to listen to. She made it out to be almost an adventure, something exciting. Not for me though. I had Sheridan, I didn't need anything else.

When the men came back, the same conversation continued. How Erica managed her day, the quality clients she had picked up over the years, how she handled inappropriate behaviour, the money she made. A combination of the dope and the alcohol meant that I wasn't thinking straight. So I didn't see it coming.

'What do you think then?' asked Sheridan.

'What do you mean?'

'You. Going out with Erica on the streets?'

'What?! What do you mean, darling?'

'I want you on the streets, girl.'

'No way,' I chuckled nervously. 'Stop teasing me. Why would you want me to do that? You sell cars, you're not a pimp!'

Garth laughed hard and long. Erica just smiled awkwardly.

'You mean you are?! You've been lying to me! What ... Why did you do that? I thought you loved me!'

'Sure babe. I love you all the way to the bank.'

I got up to leave. Garth moved to the door to block the way.

'Let me go, Garth. Let me out. I'm leaving.'

'You're not going anywhere just now darling,' Sheridan said, as he put his arms around me. I pushed him away. He pushed back. I fell into Garth's arms.

'Sit down, Linda, and I'll tell you how it is.'

Kidnapped

It turns out Sheridan had been a pimp for years. He had 'recruited' me. There was no love there. Our friendship with Garth and Erica had been part of the recruitment. The dope was to ease me in to the lifestyle.

I was a bit doped up, but not enough to misunderstand. 'This is kidnapping, Sheridan! You can't do this! I'm not interested.'

'I don't care whether you are interested or not. It's what you'll be doing from now on. If you want to live that is.'

I heard the words. Slowly it dawned. This wasn't violence in the way I had suffered it with Terry. This was worse. Modern slavery. He knew I had nowhere to go. He knew he could find me if I tried to run.

I pretended to be brave: 'I'm going now. We can talk about it tomorrow.' Garth blocked the door again.

'You ain't goin' nowhere, honey.'

I turned towards the back of the flat, but before I got out of the side door, Sheridan was there, pinning me to the wall.

'Let me show you something,' he said. He half-carried me out to the balcony of their third storey flat.

'Look, that's your new patch. A whole world out there for you, Linda.'

I struggled to break free, but there was no way. His arms were strong.

'Will you do it?'

'No I won't! Let me go!'

In an instant, he had lifted me off the floor, turned me upside down and held me by my feet, over the balcony. It was a long way down.

'Don't, Sheridan! You're hurting me. Put me down.'

'Sure, babe, I'll put you down. I'll drop you. It will look like an accident. No way will you survive the fall.'

'No! Don't!' I screamed.

'Scream all you want, babe. Ain't no one comin' to save ya. Now tell me you'll go on the streets and I'll put you down.'

'No!' I was reaching out with my hands, trying to grab hold of the railings, but Sheridan had me too far out from the edge. He was strong. He'd done this before.

'Last chance. I'm gonna drop ya. After three. Three. Two...'

'Alright, alright. I'll do it! Just don't drop me!'

He lifted me back in, laughing, carried me back into the flat, threw me onto the sofa. Garth and Erica were still there. Garth was smiling. Erica had tears in her eyes.

'I'm so, so sorry Linda. I had no choice.'

Sheridan sat down, lit up another spliff, acted as if nothing had happened. I was shaking uncontrollably, curled up in a ball, crying all the while.

'Okay darling, take this, it will calm you down. Now we'll talk about it in the morning.'

Sheridan and Garth left. Erica tried to hold me. I wouldn't let her. In the end I fell asleep, waking in the early hours of the morning to a life of slavery.

In Deep

It turns out Sheridan was known in the city, not only as a pimp, but as a drug dealer. Over the next few days, he took me to various houses he owned. I had no idea of this side of his life. I met many other girls in the same situation as me. All pretty much high on dope or worse. All caught in prostitution and knowing they would be beaten up if they tried to escape.

'Stay with me a while,' said Erica. 'I'll show you how it's done'. That was the start, out on the street. Sheridan gave me a terraced house to work from on Derby Road. I had my own 'special' room, all beautifully done out.

Sometimes we were on the street. Other times, as the clients began to know about me, all I had to do was wait for them to call. The light in the hallway was red. When it was switched on, it meant I was available.

I saw what happened to girls who tried to escape. There was a rumour one had even been killed. I was frightened, more alone than ever. Sheridan left the speed (amphetamine) on the kitchen table. He knew I would use it.

I drank it with water at first. Then, when I began to get addicted to amphetamines, I'd snort it too. That was more instant, although it damaged my nose. But it made me feel good. Mellow, relaxed. Able to cope. It was the only way I knew to get through the days and weeks on the street.

Six months into the game and I was on heroin. One of the other girls had some and I was feeling low. I'd not injected before. It hurt, of course, but the rush was good. Life didn't feel so bad after all. I was bringing in good money. Sheridan let me keep some and the drugs were free. He knew that was his noose around my neck. Run from him and no drugs. The thought of the lack of drugs tightened around me, choking my freedom, strangling any desire to go anywhere.

Some of the clients offered me a way out. Some of them genuinely cared. But I was trapped, too afraid. A drug addict, a prostitute, lost and alone. How did it come to this?

Fear

I still lived with Sheridan on occasion. He actually had two or three of us he treated as partners in his bed. We tried to avoid him, but you really had no choice.

Sheridan became violent once he knew I no longer cared for him. He began to beat me up just for the sake of it. It was best to keep quiet. If you argued with him, even if you were right, you were in for a beating.

One time, we got a 'red' reminder from the phone company for an unpaid bill. I had told Sheridan to pay it, reminded him a couple of times, but when the red bill came, I got the blame. Beaten up again.

Sheridan would usually stay in bed on Saturday morning. I went shopping usually, but not for too long. If I was out for too long, I would be accused of visiting friends or of doing business behind his back. Another beating.

I told my friends it was a bad customer. The truth is, it was Sheridan every time. I was afraid to do anything that might upset him. Afraid not to work the streets.

Months passed. Years passed. Nearly six years in all. Six years of abuse, drugs and prostitution.

Was it worth living?

Life's Gone

It was late on a Friday night when I did it. I'd had some news that week that wrecked me. Terry had agreed to the children going into foster care. Phil and his wife had tried to keep them, but they couldn't cope. I had wanted to go and see them, but I was in slavery, deep into drugs, with no escape and no hope.

When the social worker left, I took heroin. I dosed up high. The downer was hard. I shook physically, cried all the time. What was the use? What was there to live for if Georgie and Matt were gone? My life had gone. There was nothing left. That Friday, I gathered all the prescription drugs I had, sat on the floor by the bed, lined up the pills next to one another, said a prayer and swallowed them all.

Did I mean it? Did I want to die?

I really don't know. You see, I had left the door open. I took an overdose of prescription drugs, not of heroin. It was only a matter of time before a client found me. He got me to hospital and my stomach was pumped out. Sheridan came to see me. He wanted me to know that he cared. But I couldn't help feeling that underlying his concern was a clearer message:

'Don't think you can escape through this; I want you back on the streets.'

Back on the street, I lived day to day, fixing myself with heroin, trying to avoid Sheridan but tending to my clients. I was in a permanent daze. My girlfriends stopped calling. I would just sit there. As one fix wore off, I took another. I had little idea what day of the week it was and measured time by way of light and darkness, sleep and work. A second overdose followed. The pattern was the same. Discovered in time, stomach pumped out. A few days in hospital, then back to the streets.

Jesus Loves You

I saw them across the street, speaking with Carol, another prostitute. Then they came over to me. I thought they were lost and asking for directions. That was before they began to talk.

'Hello, I'm Toni, this is Karen.'

Two black ladies, well dressed with big smiles.

'No thanks. No. I'm not interested.'

'You don't know what we are going to say, dear.'

'Yes I do. You're Jehovah's Witnesses.'

They smiled. 'No we're not. We're from the New Testament Church of God on Ivy Road. We've been watching you. We think we can help.'

'How?'

'First of all, we want to pray for you. We want you to know that Jesus loves you.'

'What? I'm a prostitute. How could Jesus want anything to do with someone like me?'

Their smiles widened. 'You are exactly the kind of person Jesus is interested in. Matthew 21 says tax collectors and prostitutes are more likely to get into God's kingdom than the well off and religious.' I wasn't clear who Matthew was and why his age of 21 was important. But there was something about the ladies that made me want to know more.

'I can't talk now. I've got to ... work. But, call again. That's my house over there. If the red light's on, I'm not with a client. You can call.'

I said it to get rid of them, really.

'Oh yes, we will. We'll call,' they said. Little did I know how persistent they would be!

I met Toni and Karen a few times after that, but only for a few snatched minutes here and there. I was afraid Sheridan would find me with them. I didn't want another beating. One question they kept asking stayed with me.

'Why don't you run away? Why don't you escape?'

I'd been afraid to try, but something in their plea to me struck home. Maybe I could? Maybe there was a way out?

Chapter 6
All The Time
In The World

Maybe. Just maybe. The words of hope spoken by Toni and Karen stayed with me. 'Your life can change. Why don't you escape? It can't be that impossible.' Other friends said it too. Especially when they saw the bruises.

I had tried early on. A few times. Before I got addicted to heroin. But Sheridan had caught me pretty easily. Sometimes there was a beating, sometimes a fake concern. But always back on the streets.

Then heroin had taken over. I was so dosed up, I never really thought about it. For the best part of six years, I never really thought about it. Six years. As I write this, it feels impossible that I had stayed that long. But that's modern slavery for you. A drug induced haze gets you through the days. Violence, or the threat of it, keeps you from running. I let the days go. I let hope disappear. I let others take over my life.

A particularly bad argument with Sheridan one day led to another beating. Something snapped with me. The pain was so intense, it broke through the drugs. This, combined with the words of encouragement spoken by friends, got me to the point of trying again.

Escape

I planned my moves carefully. Be nice to Sheridan. Work hard. Bring in more income than usual. Pack a small bag. Keep it hidden. I had arranged for a lift with Angela. She was another prostitute in Southampton, but she worked for someone else. Someone who let her travel away at weekends.

Late at night, I left by the back door. Through the alleys and out into another area of the city. Angela was waiting for me. We were to drive to Bristol, one hundred and three long miles away, where she had a small flat.

I remember the journey. The car was hot, but I was shivering. A mix of not having had a fix and the sheer fear of being caught. Sheridan had so ruled my life, it was hard to think for myself.

We arrived in Bristol early in the morning. The clouds were grey and the wind cold. But by then, my fear had subsided. I was excited. My blood was pumping. This was it! I had done it! Escaped from nearly six years of slavery.

Angie's flat was in one of the poorer areas of Bristol, St Paul's. It was an area the council seemed to have forgotten about. Boarded over windows, vandalised shop fronts. And drugs. Drugs big time. Heroin and crack cocaine were traded in broad daylight. All of it run by gangs, who when they weren't shooting up, were fighting turf wars. Not the most comfortable of places to stay, but anywhere was better than the slavery I had been in.

'Just going down to the caff for cigarettes, Angie. Anything you want?'

'No thanks. See ya later.'

That was the last I saw of Angie in a long time. As I queued in the café, there was a familiar voice behind me.

'Well, well. What have we here? Hello Linda. Fancy meeting you.'

Before I could move, I felt something digging into my ribs. Garth had pulled a gun. There was an inane grin on his face. I stood still. Forgot to breathe. This was a nightmare, surely?

It was the strangest of feelings. I still remember it today. It felt completely unreal. I was so afraid, I thought I might faint. At the same time, adrenaline was pumping. My mind was working fast. How had they found me? How could I escape? What would be the consequences of being caught?

'What's the gun for, Garth? Why are you holding a gun? It's me, Linda.' I was shaking by now. Uncontrollably. Garth could hear the quiver in my voice. 'I'm just visiting with a friend for the weekend.'

'You don't get to visit anyone, babe. You've run away. Now, move. I want you to turn around, walk out of the café and over to my car – the blue Jaguar. You get in and you sit still. Sheridan will be pleased with this find, that's for sure!'

Within the hour, I was in the back of a car, being taken back to Southampton, my hands tied behind me, two of Garth's friends either side.

It was one of those chance things. Garth and his friends had been over, doing some drug deals. They had called into the café at the very same moment.

The gun had shaken me up. No one had done that to me before. I knew I was in serious trouble.

'You're My Girl!'

It was early evening by the time we got back. The traffic around Southampton was slow. I tried to chat to Garth and his friends, to joke with them. They didn't speak more than a few words the whole journey. I could see Garth's two friends were high. But Garth was as sharp as anything. I could see the glint in his eyes. There was no doubt that his find would help him within the strict management hierarchy that Sheridan ran. A neat little bonus too, no doubt.

By the time we got to Sheridan's house, I had decided on my tactics. I was going to lie and say my friend was ill. She needed company for a few days. I had to go there. She needed me. I was going to come back, of course I was. No, I would never run away. How could I?

I didn't get to try and explain.

Garth had phoned ahead from Bristol. Sheridan was expecting me. He untied my hands and asked Garth and his friends to leave. That wasn't good. I'd found Sheridan to be more violent when there weren't any witnesses.

Garth closed the front door to the house and all three went back to the car. I tried to look Sheridan in the eye, begin my speech. Before I'd got into the first sentence, there was a slap across the face. It shook me up.

'Come in here.'

Through into the back dining room. Good thinking, Sheridan. No one could look in. Less likely anyone would hear the screams. My face was hurting, but I knew from experience that was just the beginning.

As I stepped into the dining room, Sheridan reached over, dragged me in, shut the door.

'Why? Why, babe? Why'd you do that to me?'

'I was just...'

The blow came in from the side. It winded me and put me on the floor. Then a kick across my back. I was dragged back to my feet.

'Don't lie. You lie, I'll make you a cripple.'

'I... I'm sorry... I didn't mean...'

Another punch. Again into my side. I'm on the floor again. Crying now. My brave face has crumpled. The lies I had prepared were forgotten.

He lifted me up. Held me by the shoulders. Lifted my face up and forced me to look at him.

'What am I to do, Linda? If I'm soft on you, the other girls will know. You realise that, don't you? Don't you, Linda? Say you realise that.'

I nodded slowly.

'Well, we can't be harming this beautiful face can we? No, that wouldn't do at all.'

It happened so quickly, I didn't really feel much pain. A hard punch to my stomach winded me. A number of blows to the body. As I fell to the floor, kick after kick followed. Sheridan was shouting. Screaming that I wasn't to do it again. That he'd kill me. That he loved his 'girls'. That he'd look after me if I was a good girl.

'You're my girl! You're my girl!' he kept shouting.

At some stage, I lost consciousness. I came round much later. It was dark, but the streetlamp outside showed me I had been dumped back in my house. I was on the floor of the lounge.

All was not well. Intense pain was pulsing through my body. I had blood in my mouth, but no facial injuries. Internal bleeding.

Not good.

I tried to move. There was an overpowering pain below my rib cage, on the left side of my body. I fainted.

I don't think I was out for long. But I knew when I came round again that things were serious. If I didn't get an ambulance, I wasn't sure I would make it.

Taking deep breaths, I slowly dragged myself to the phone. Thankfully it was in the lounge, just a few feet from where I lay. It was a ruptured spleen. My case was so serious, I had to be transferred to a specialist unit at Poole Hospital, 40 miles away. Or that's what they said. I wonder now whether someone was being clever, realising I had been beaten up and trying to put me out of harm's way.

All The Time In The World

The first few days in hospital were not good. The operation was successful – they managed to save my spleen. But there were no drugs in hospital. I was on 'cold turkey'. I could have explained, could have asked for methadone, a prescription substitute for heroin, but I didn't want to draw attention to myself. It was bad enough the police being involved. The usual questions. My usual answers. Even then, I covered up. I didn't want to help the police. I didn't want them digging into my history either.

'You've got visitors, Linda.'

Fear.

My immediate thought was that it would be Sheridan or Garth. Perhaps the police again – nearly as bad.

'Hi, my lovely. We've brought you some flowers.'

The unmistakeable smiles of Toni and Karen. How I'd come to love them!

Looking back over the years, I know why I loved them so much. There was no judgement. No accusing finger. No manipulation, pretend love, other motives. They just cared. It was a rare thing for me. For someone to say 'we care for you' without there being a motive behind it was pretty unknown for me at that time. Sure, they wanted to share their faith. But there was more to them than that. There was genuine love and compassion. They were feeling how I felt, not just saying it. And to travel 40 miles to see me, that was some friendship.

After a few preliminaries, Toni beamed at me.

'Hey, guess what!'

'What?'

'You were always telling us you didn't have time to talk with us for long. Well, you have now. We have all the time in the world!'

And we did. I wasn't going anywhere and they were willing to stay as long as the hospital allowed them. I was so glad to see them. Their care for me went deep inside. I found it to be a healing thing. I felt better for them being there.

'Linda, we know what you need. Will you give us permission to talk to you about our faith?'

'Yes. Of course. Yes.'

Over the next hour or so, first Karen and then Toni told me of their lives. How God was real to them. How someone called Jesus really did exist. History showed it, they said. And He wasn't just a good man. He was God's son. His death on the cross was to take my place and theirs. We deserved death, but He gave us life. So the impossible was possible. Even someone like me could know God personally. I could pray. I could ask forgiveness. I could ask Jesus to change my life.

As I listened, my heart beat faster. I paid attention. This was for real. This was the God who had been with my mother. A God who was with her to the very end. This was a personal, life-changing faith.

Karen showed me a few Bible verses. How Jesus had dealt with the prostitutes, the outcasts. Me. That was me. I could see myself in the stories.

'This is real isn't it?'

'Yes Linda, this is real.'

I couldn't kneel, couldn't move really, but I held Toni and Karen's hands as they led me in a simple prayer. They spoke it, I repeated it.

'Lord Jesus, I know You are alive and are still changing lives today. Please change mine. Forgive me, Lord, for my life lived without You. I invite You in right now as my Lord and Saviour. Please come and change me. Amen.'

I felt clean. For the first time since my childhood, I felt clean. It was as if God had taken away every hurt, every harmful thought, every bad thing that had happened to me. I was crying. But tears of joy. For the first time in a long time, tears of joy. The thrill that God loved me. That He had changed me. That He had answered that specific prayer. I was laughing and crying at the same time. Tears were running down Toni and Karen's faces. We were laughing together. Goodness – what must the nurses have thought!

It was a strange thing to think. A strange thing to say.

'This is better than drugs,' I said. 'This is a real high!'

Toni smiled.

'We need to pray for God's protection on you, Linda. What you are feeling is God working in you by His Holy Spirit. That's the feeling. But whatever happens, long after these feelings, you will still know God's love and protection in a new way. That's our prayer for you.'

And so they prayed again. I felt like I was in God's arms. Like a small child on her Father's lap, curled up, safe. Safe. That was a word I hadn't used for a while. Safe.

Then they prayed again. This time for the healing of my body. I felt heat go right through me. I actually looked up to see what had happened, but there were Toni and Karen praying away, eyes closed. What was the heat?! It had to be God at work. It certainly wasn't my imagination.

Toni and Karen left the ward eventually. But I still felt safe. And still felt a heat on my body. I knew God had done a miracle. Jesus had changed me. He had accepted me. A prostitute. A drug user. No condemnation. Just love.

A Healing God

It felt unreal. There was a strength in my body I'd not known for many years. Just a prayer. That's all it had been.

Slowly, very slowly, I eased myself out of the hospital bed and into a standing position. No pain. A few minutes before I'd been doubled over, but now, here I was, standing straight.

It was impulsive – reaching for the vase of flowers, I took out the biggest, the most beautiful. Carefully cradling the yellow petals, I began to walk. Out of the ward. Down the corridor. Through to the Chapel. There, at the front, by the altar, I laid down the flower.

'Thank you God.' It was all I could say at first. And then, as my thoughts returned to the situation I was in, 'Help me God. Help me. It feels like I'm in a dark place, God. I don't want to go back to the streets. But right now I'm afraid. If I run, I'll get beaten up again. But how can I do anything else? Help me God. Help me.'

I looked up. Bright sunlight. The sun shone through the high windows, reflecting the yellow flower on the white table top.

Maybe, just maybe. If God has got me this far... Maybe tomorrow can be different?

Chapter 7
The Man In The Night

It was a slow recovery, but in the end I was discharged and back to the life I lived. Back to Southampton. Back on the streets.

I didn't dare tell Sheridan what had happened to me. I was still in fear. But there were changes. Not least, Toni and Karen being around. They called all the time now. Often they would bring their knitting with them. They knew that I would turn men away if they were there – so they camped out!

Not that they could stay all the time. I still had to make enough money to keep on the right side of Sheridan. But things were so different. I felt I couldn't live this life any more. I felt dirty if I was with a man. I knew it was wrong. But what to do?

Finally, I plucked up the courage. I told Sheridan I had changed. That Jesus was real. That I had God helping me in my life now.

'You'll need God's help if you don't get back on those streets now!' Said with a smile. But the menace was still there.

The fear returned. What was it to be this time? Another six years on the streets? Being beaten up whenever he felt like it? Panic. Fear. All the old feelings were there. After just one confrontation. What was I to do?

Freedom

There was one other major difference though. It really was a big one. I was off drugs. For the first time in years, I was clean. And I didn't want them, didn't crave them. God had done a work. An amazing work. I'd started to come off them in hospital. And then from the moment I had prayed that prayer – nothing! No craving. No desire to go back there. In one moment, I had been made free. Free to live the life God wanted. And free from drugs!

There may have been fear still, especially when I was around Sheridan. But there was hope too. I really was different. So different, it didn't take me long to begin to plan a further escape. And with my mind clearer, this would be better planned and to a place where no one would find me.

The moment came within a few months of my return. Sheridan had to go to Wales to sort out a drug deal. I knew this was my best chance. With a clearer head and off drugs, I was thinking logically. I had to go somewhere where he could never find me. It couldn't be Angie in Bristol. It couldn't be with Erica or any of my friends from the streets.

One thing I had kept secret from Sheridan was the whereabouts of my family. I didn't want him to know. He wasn't the kind of man you would want to introduce to anyone, anyway. And conversely, I didn't want my family knowing about me either. They may have guessed, I supposed, but I had never told them I was a prostitute.

I packed all I could. Called a cab. Said goodbye to Toni and Karen. And went.

As we drove out of the city, I looked back at the street lights, shining orange in the night. Six years of my life. Six years of slavery. Of a drug-induced haze. Red lights rather than orange. But no more. I felt my jaw tensing up as I looked back. Tense. A little fearful. But determined as well. Only Toni and Karen knew where I was going. Safety. A future. A plan.

The taxi drove all the way to Spalding in Lincolnshire. I was sure my brother Paul and his wife Joy wouldn't mind looking after me for a few weeks while I found my feet.

We arrived about 1.00 in the morning. I hadn't called Paul in advance. I was paranoid that somehow Sheridan would be able to trace the call. Maybe I had been watching too many cop shows on television, but the fear of him was so intense, I didn't want to do anything that could lead him to me. He had so many contacts too. He had said to me that if I ran away, someone would always find me. So no loose ends this time.

After Paul had got over the shock, given the cab driver a cup of tea (thinking he was my boyfriend for the first few minutes!) and settled me in, I began to explain enough to him to get his agreement to stay.

'Of course you can stay. As long as you want. It's so good to see you, Linda!' Words of love. There had been so few over the years. I cried.

Hospital again

I wasn't able to start job searching as I had planned, as pretty much straight away, I had to go into hospital at nearby Boston. Complications from the beating Sheridan had given me.

Even now, I was in fear of Sheridan finding me. I gave instructions to Paul and Joy before I left for the hospital that if a black guy called looking for me, they were not to say anything about me. Not to tell him that I was with them. So it was a tearful Joy that called the hospital one night and said that indeed, a black guy had called and she had not been able to lie. He was on his way.

Fear and panic again. I called the nurse, explained the problem. She alerted security. It was quite late at night by then, so visitors would not be allowed anyway. She assured me that when the person arrived, there was no doubt he would be sorted out and sent on his way.

A few minutes later and the nurse looked puzzled. 'Linda, are you sure this man is who you think he is?'

'Yes nurse, he is. He seems nice enough, doesn't he? But he wants me back with him. Call the police if he comes here again. Please. Don't let him get to me!'

'Okay, if you say so. Doesn't seem to be so bad though. He told security he was a church pastor!'

'Well, that's a new one. He's just trying to get through to me. He knows I have a new faith.'

'Alright. Sleep well.'

I couldn't sleep. Eventually, when I did, back came the dreams of being on the street. I saw Angie and Erica and my other friends from the streets, smiling, laughing, inviting me to join them. Then I saw them again, this time caught in chains. Again, in my dream, I was there as well, running from Sheridan, fighting him off. I woke in a cold sweat. But it was alright. I was still in the hospital. The nurse was still there, at the end of the ward. All was well. Sleep at last.

I woke the next morning with the conversation with the nurse running through my head. 'Are you sure this man is who you think it is?' I asked about him again when the same nurse came back on duty that evening. 'The strange thing is,' she said, 'he seemed so nice. He kept saying his name is Michael and he's a pastor.'

For two evenings he kept calling and for two evenings I kept him away. I started to joke with the nurses that he was my 'man in the night'!

But the insistence was unusual. Sheridan was always so busy. He wouldn't wait around for me, would he? It didn't sound like him. He'd be more likely to get one of his henchmen to stay; wait outside the hospital until I came out. Eventually, my inquisitiveness overcame my fear.

'Hello Linda. I'm Pastor Michael from the New Testament Church of God in Peterborough. Your friends Toni and Karen called me. I've been travelling over each evening waiting to see you.'

'Oh, Pastor. I.... I'm so sorry!'

He smiled. Such a gentle smile. No irritation with me. Just that gentle look, that smile. As I look back over the years, it's what you remember about Pastor Michael. The smile. It could break through the hardest of hearts.

Pastor Michael was a lovely young man in in his early thirties, confident, purposeful – and persistent! The fact he had driven every night from Peterborough, a round trip of around seventy miles, and had been so persistent, showed me straight away how much he cared. Here was someone I could trust.

'So when are you out of here?'

'Thursday, I hope.'

'Come and stay with us if you want. Karen said you were with your brother, but were a bit worried about overcrowding him.'

'Paul and Joy are great, but yes, there's not a lot of room. But why, Pastor Michael? Why do you want to help me? I'm a mess. I've been a prostitute, on drugs most of the time, an alcoholic too.'

'That's okay, Linda. That was then. This is now.'

That smile again. My past really didn't bother him. Such acceptance. More tears.

And so, my move to Peterborough.

Starting Over

It was the strangest thing, starting over. I'd not had to make any decisions for years. They were all made for me. And if I had been allowed to make decisions, the effect of being permanently on drugs stopped any clear thinking.

But here I was, in Peterborough. And thanks to Pastor Michael, with the possibility of a flat on Oundle Road. It was only a two-room apartment on the ground floor, but it was a start. The problem was, the landlord Pastor Michael introduced me to wanted a deposit. I explained my dilemma to the Pastor.

'Why don't you pray about it, Linda?'

Not something I'd done much of over the years. How exactly was I meant to pray anyway? The first thing I did was buy a Bible. I figured that I needed to know a bit about the guy I was praying to! I bought a children's Bible. It seemed the quickest way to get into the stories.

Then armed with the children's Bible, I settled down to pray. Should I kneel? I supposed so. Hands together like in the picture on the front? Okay. 'Dear Lord, I need some money please. (Do you say 'please' when you pray, Lord? Sorry, silly question.) Well, there it is, Lord. What do I do now?'

I waited. As sure as hearing a voice, I felt I heard the Lord say to look around me. 'What do You mean, "look around you"?'

I waited for a reply.

Nothing.

I opened my eyes, allowed my hands to part from their prayer position and looked. It was there. Right in front of me! There, on my hands! Gold. Loads of it. Rings on every finger. Bracelets too. Sheridan's gifts through the years. No way did I want to keep it all anyway.

A trip to a dealer's and the deposit was paid for the first two months. 'Lord, I like this praying thing!'

The next few weeks seemed like another world. It was another world. People who loved and cared for me. Church on Sunday. Meals out with members of the congregation. People praying for me. I had been so starved of love for so long, the whole thing felt unreal. I cried a lot during those days. God did a lot of healing, constantly bringing the right people across my path to help me and pray with me.

But you have to be careful too, as to whom your friends are, especially when you've been in the kind of bad places I had. I wasn't careful enough.

Back Into The Dark

When you've been an alcoholic, it's not wise to work in a pub. But that's where I found myself with one of my characteristic moments of not thinking straight. I needed the money to pay the rent and I figured I could always find a better job when one came along.

Beth, the owner of The Lion, began to introduce me to her own set of friends. Fitzroy was one of them. He was Rastafarian by background; long plaited hair, mischievous eyes and a big smile. It wasn't long before we were dating. And it wasn't long before I was back smoking dope.

Slowly my links with Pastor Michael and his church lessened. Clubbing and drinking took the place of time with the church family. I enjoyed Fitzroy's company too. It was hard for me not to have a boyfriend. It was what I'd been used to. I felt I needed a man in my life. I felt so insecure on my own. And, as always seemed to be the case, I wasn't too careful who I picked.

Amsterdam

'I'm going to Amsterdam with Leroy. We could do with a driver, Linda, will you come?'

'Oh, that would be nice. I've never been there.'

Fitzroy's invitation was not for a vacation though. He was trading cannabis and Leroy was a known drug dealer from nearby Wellingborough.

I said 'no'.

Later in the week I heard the news. My long term friend from the streets, Erica, had died. A drug overdose.

I was so low, so upset.

'Bye Linda, we're on our way to Amsterdam.'

'Fitzroy, wait for me, I'm coming.' I needed his company, so I agreed to drive.

All went well in Amsterdam. The deal was done and I even got to see some of the sights. Our ferry was scheduled to arrive back into Dover in the early evening. Again, no problems with Amsterdam customs and the journey over was quite enjoyable. Leroy stayed on the ferry as a foot passenger and said he would meet us outside the docks. We didn't even think to ask why he would do that. Both Fitzroy and I were tense as we drove off the slipway. Not a word was said. My mouth was dry. I began to shake slightly at the thought of what we were doing. But surely, all would be fine. We had managed the Amsterdam end without an issue. It would be the same here. I waited in the queue, slowly edging forwards towards the custom point.

We noticed the customs officials staring at each of the cars. As soon as they saw us, they called us over. I was nervous and they could see it. Not helped by the fact that I hit the accelerator at one point, rather than the brake and nearly ran one of them over!

'Hello sir, madam. Can you tell me where you have been today?'

'Amsterdam,' I said.

'Belgium,' Fitzroy said simultaneously.

A frown on the customs official's face.

'We mean both, of course!' Fitzroy said quickly.

'May we have a look inside your vehicle please, madam?'

'Yes, of course.'

I was visibly shaking now. They could see it.

'Step out of the vehicle please, sir and madam.'

It took the sniffer dogs all of two minutes to find the stash, not-so-secretly hidden. Two kilos of cannabis.

Leroy was picked up at the roundabout. It turns out he had been under surveillance for some weeks. They found another thirty-three kilos at his house. And their assumption was that Fitzroy and I were part of the same gang. It wasn't even a hire car we had been driving, it was Leroy's. We were advised at the court in Bedford that bail would not be offered and I was told I would be taken away to a women's prison to await trial.

As Fitzroy was escorted out of another entrance, I felt very alone. And very foolish. I thought of saying a prayer, but wasn't sure I was allowed to pray when I had willingly taken part in a criminal activity.

An arm on my shoulder.

'Come on, love.'

I was taken to the van, ready for my move to prison. Holloway prison, Islington, London. Home of notorious women prisoners. And now home to one rather timid and fearful new inmate.

As the van turned onto the main road, I closed my eyes. 'Please Lord. I don't deserve it, but please Lord, help me out of this mess.'

Chapter 8
All You Have To
Do Is Ask

The crash of steel on steel. The slow realisation that I was on the inside of those enormous doors.

On the inside. It hit me hard. What a fool I'd been. I'd begun to do the right things. I'd found a faith and good friends. And in a bout of insecurity, I had traded it in for dope and a crooked boyfriend. I had screwed up. Those were the words going through my head. I'd screwed up big time.

'Are these all your possessions?'

Confronting me was a female prison officer over six feet tall and looking like a man! If the prison had chosen who should deal with the newcomers, they had chosen wisely.

'Yes,' I said.

'It's "Yes Miss" to you!' she shouted.

I visibly quaked in front of her, much to the amusement of some of the long term prisoners who were helping.

There is no easy first day in prison. As we handed in our belongings, I felt it was not just my possessions that were being taken away, but my dignity too. We had to take our clothes off and put on a medical gown. After a bath and hair wash, we were shown in to a nurse who did various medical checks. Then into the prison itself, wearing a few of our own clothes that were given back to us.

Because I was due back in court, I was kept on D3 block. This was basically a processing area for prisoners coming and going. It's an old prison and the rooms are pretty basic. Mine was a small room with bunk beds, a small table and a screened off area for a toilet and hand basin. That was it. This was to be my new home.

An hour into my stay, the cell door opened and another prisoner was shown in. Sandy told me she was in for beating up an old man. I reasoned that I was not as bad as that, so what was I doing here? Feeling sorry for myself, I cried myself to sleep that night. Silent crying of course, in case Sandy heard me and decided to beat me up too.

Processing continued the next day. I was interviewed by the governor – a formidable lady who scared me just by looking at me. Then we all received a Gideon's Bible and filled in various forms. This included a form where you identified any food allergies. One of the prisoners helping us new girls had whispered to me to put down that I was a vegetarian, because the meat was so bad. That's what I did and, as the weeks went by and I saw the prison food, it turned out to be one of the wisest things I'd done! Back in court, I was found guilty, had a charge of soliciting added to the list, from my Southampton days, and was sent back to Holloway. The sentence was for twenty-one months, but I served eleven months before being let out.

The first few weeks back in Holloway were lonely.

I was cold a lot of the time and even doing duties around the prison didn't really break the monotony. I prayed occasionally. 'God, if you're real, hear me, get me out. I promise I'll never do anything like this again.'

No answer. 'He's forgotten me,' I reasoned. God had given me one chance. That was it. I'd blown it and He wasn't going to give me another. Or at least, that's what I thought.

All You Have To Do Is Ask

'Good morning ladies, how are we today?'

It was Snowy, our prison officer, unlocking our door for the day. She got her nickname due to the bleached blonde colour of her hair.

'What's the matter, Linda, you look sad?'

'So would you, if you were this side of the door!'

'I see you've been reading the Gideon's Bible,' she said, pointing to the book on the table.

'Yes, just a bit. Doesn't make sense though.'

'It does if you ask God to help you read it.'

'What?' I said. I was surprised by Snowy's reply. I wasn't sure the guards were meant to talk about their faith.

'All you have to do is ask.'

She smiled. There was a definite twinkle in her eye.

I became fascinated by Snowy. Her attitude to the prisoners was different to most. She treated us with respect. She seemed to genuinely care for us. Her parting comment stayed with me. Ask *what*? All I have to do is ask for what?

Joel

I was struggling with something else too. My landlord, not

unreasonably, was wanting me out. I had paid some rent, but he wasn't sure he wanted a jailbird in his flats. But without a home, it would be hard to get parole. They always wanted you to have somewhere of your own to go. I asked to see someone in the prison that could help.

'Hi. My name is Joel Edwards. I'm your designated Probation Officer. If I can help you I will.'

I explained the problem. A phone call to Pastor Michael and the problem was solved. It turned out that Joel worked part time in the prison. He was also a pastor and knew Pastor Michael in Peterborough.

Maybe God was giving me a second chance after all?

I met Joel a couple of times after that. He was able to pray with me and slowly but surely, I found my fledgling faith rekindled.

Joel introduced me to Alethea, a prison visitor. Alethea was a little lady with a gentle voice and a very funny childlike giggle. And such confidence! She made up for her small size with loads of personality. I would see her arriving in the visitors' area and I began to look forward to her visits. As soon as I heard her giggling in the distance, there would be an excitement, an anticipation of her visit. She would bustle through to the visitors' room, beaming all over her face.

'Linda!' (giggle) 'How are you? You're looking well!' Always the encourager. Gentle voice. Gentle smile. Gentle heart.

I wasn't well though. Further complications from the beating I had from Sheridan meant I was back in hospital with guards on the door. Alethea followed me there. She would only ever stay a few minutes, but they were such quality times. We would pray together and Alethea would always leave me with deep questions to answer.

I Can't Forgive Myself

News came through of my grandfather's death and I was allowed out for the funeral. I had always been close to him and my gran. To an extent, they had looked after me and kept in touch once my mum died.

But the funeral wasn't until 4.00pm and I had to be back in Holloway for 7.00pm, so I was whisked away at the end, without even a moment to be with Gran. I felt so ashamed and sorry for myself. Angry with myself too, for letting all this happen. And just when my gran needed me, I wasn't there for her.

I told Alethea about it on her next visit. I was tearful and spouting a load of rubbish about not forgiving myself. Suddenly, the gentle smile was gone. Alethea looked stern, stood up; all five foot of her looking down at me!

'Linda! Are you saying that even though God has forgiven you, you can't forgive yourself? Have you become bigger than God all of a sudden? Who are you to say you can't be forgiven? God has said it, Jesus has done it!'

I was shocked. But in a good way. It came to be another turning point for me.

The Library

I reasoned that if I was to make something of my faith, I needed to learn more about it. My Bible was being read, but I didn't understand a lot of it.

When I was over in another wing of the prison, I found a book someone had left there. They had written in the front that it was a good read until you got to the 'God' bit. I was intrigued and started to read. The more I read, the more I wanted to read. The book was called *Run, Baby, Run* by Nicky Cruz. A gang leader in

New York, he was radically converted. Here was a murderer who found forgiveness! God loved him. I was deeply affected by what I read. It was going to be okay. It was possible to start again. God did love me.

In its pages I found stories of prostitutes too. Girls like me. Just like Nicky Cruz they came to a real living faith. Not just a belief, but one that was worked out in a new, radical lifestyle. That's what I wanted. That's what I needed. If God did it for those girls, then why not me?

I read through the night and was in tears by the morning. God was changing my whole mind-set. I may have been in prison, but He was setting me free on the inside. Hope was rising. I didn't need to go down the old avenues any more. It wasn't inevitable I would go back to drugs or drink. I could change dramatically, just like Nicky. Just like the prostitutes in the book.

I was hungry to read more. I saw another book advertised on the back of the one I was reading. It was called *The Cross and the Switchblade*. It told me that this was the story of Nicky and his friends written by the pastor that had first met them on the streets. I needed to read it. I needed to find it.

A trip to the prison library, a conversation with Jamie the librarian and an introduction to a complete shelf of Christian books. That top left shelf in the prison library changed me. I was so excited. Story after story of transformed lives. In *The Hiding Place*, God kept Corrie Ten Boom safe right through the Nazi persecution. I read of Doreen Irvine escaping from witchcraft. And of revival in Indonesia in Mel Tari's book. Rita Nightingale was imprisoned for drug smuggling in Thailand and God met her. There I was again in the pages. God loved drug smugglers!

So many books. I would commonly read all night now, unable

to put a book down. I was feeding my soul. Every story seemed to be just for me. I felt stronger, sharper, more alive. The Bible began to speak to me as well.

One day I asked God to help me to understand the Bible more. I held it in front of me and prayed. 'Lord, you have to help me. Show me what my next step is.'

I opened it at random (not something I'd particularly recommend to a new Christian, but it worked for me that day) and read from John's Gospel chapter three.

'You must be born again.'

There it was. All that Toni and Karen had explained was right there in front of me. God was showing me again.

And I prayed again – in the same way I had back in the hospital with Toni and Karen. I asked God to forgive me again. I said I wanted to return to Him. I asked Him to help me be strong.

Something changed that day in the way I read the Bible. Suddenly it made so much more sense.

I asked Joel for a 'real Bible'.

'But you've got one from the Gideons,' he said.

'No. It's just a New Testament. I want the real thing!'

And so I began to study. Alethea bought me Bible study courses out of her own pocket. Chaplain Hugh, who led the Prison Chapel meetings, paid for a correspondence course. Book after book. Essay after essay. Deep into the Bible. Old Testament and New. Studying on salvation, worship, church, grace, healing, praying ... So many topics, so much to learn!

Chasing the Dragon

But there was one book that particularly bothered me. *Chasing the Dragon* by Jackie Pullinger is the story of a girl travelling to

Hong Kong and seeing the hardest criminals and the worst drug addicts changed. One chapter just didn't make sense though. Jackie talked about being 'baptised in the Spirit' and 'speaking in tongues.' What on earth was speaking in tongues? It sounded weird. But it appeared to be in the Bible. So if it was on offer and it helped strengthen my faith, I wanted it!

One day I asked Snowy about it.

'Snowy, what is this thing about – speaking in tongues?'

Snowy patiently explained. A God-given language that will help me pray better, a hot-line to God, a way of asking God when I ran out of English words. And then, with a glint in her eye as always, she said her often repeated words:

'All you have to do is ask'.

And with a smile she left my cell.

I wasn't satisfied with leaving it there. By then I had my own cell, so that night I set myself to pray.

'Lord, I'm not going away until You give me this tongues thing. I want to be baptised in the Spirit. Snowy said all I had to do is ask, so I'm asking! It's in Your word; it says it's for everyone and I'm one of Your "everyone", so please give me that gift. Please baptise me in Your Holy Spirit.'

I wasn't sure what to do next, but I did feel like a word popped into my head. Was this for real? Was this tongues? Maybe it was the devil? But no, not the devil; I could feel God's presence with me. Was it just me then? Again, no. I felt God smiling at me, telling me I wasn't clever enough to make it up!

So I spoke it out.

And then another word came. And another. Before long, I was speaking in a whole new language – one I had never learned, direct from God the Holy Spirit. And there was such a presence of God in my cell that night. I felt full of the Holy Spirit. This is what baptism in the Holy Spirit is. There was a power within me. Despite praying long into the night, I felt refreshed, just like I had taken a shower.

'Lord, thank you! Thank you! THANK YOU!' I was shouting praises, intermittently speaking in tongues and in English.

'God you are so good to me! So good!'

With the power of the Holy Spirit working so obviously, I began to pray some more. For friends and family. For fellow prisoners. And with a power and authority that was completely new to me. God was real. He was with me in that cell. I could reach out and touch Him. This sounds a bit irreverent, but the nearest I can compare it to is like being high on drugs, but so much better.

And no 'downer' either, like there would be after drugs. I stayed 'high', knowing God was with me in a new, powerful way. I read and re-read the passages in the Bible. Where Peter and the disciples were filled with the Spirit and spoke in tongues. Where Cornelius and his whole household surprised Peter by speaking in tongues. Where Paul says he speaks in tongues more than anyone. It was there. In the Bible. And it had happened to me!

All I had to do was ask.

Chapter 9
The God Who Answers Prayer

My eleven months in prison were rapidly coming to an end. Shortened from the original sentence by ten months for 'good behaviour' I was grateful it was ending. But at the same time it had been a life-changing experience. And life-changing for the better – so much the opposite of many people's experience of prison.

My personal relationship with God, my understanding of Christ's salvation and my general appreciation of the Bible had grown and grown. And I was baptised in the Holy Spirit. In some ways, I was still a 'babe'. But in others, I had matured quickly. When you get stuck into God's Word, the Bible, it does amazing things. The advantage of time on your hands is that you can use it to read. Five chapters a day from the Old Testament, then five from the New Testament.

Jamie, the librarian, had noticed my hunger for Christian books and had invited me to work with her in the library as part of my appointed chores. I didn't need a second invitation.

Kelly

I had also become a regular at the Prison Fellowship meetings. The problem was, the meetings were well attended for the wrong reasons. It was an opportunity for many just to get out of their cells. They would all sit there, usually near the back, and talk. With my re-found faith, I was angry!

'Lord, you shouldn't allow this! This is not right! They are just talking, not listening. This is Your word that is being spoken. Do something Lord!'

One of the regulars – and one of the loudest talkers – was Kelly. In her forties, and a hardened criminal, she was one of those you kept away from. Seemingly as hard as nails, she wouldn't think twice about hitting you, and would regularly swear at the prison officers, even when it brought her punishment.

But it wasn't right she should disrupt the Prison Fellowship meetings with her talking. I turned around and signed for her to be quiet. Not the cleverest thing to have done. Sure enough, after the meeting, Kelly made certain I got a shove in the back for my troubles that nearly sent me sprawling. I didn't fight back though; not even a harsh word. Kelly frowned quizzically and walked off.

'Looking forward to next week then?' Snowy said, as she walked past.

'What do you mean? Hey, Snowy, stop! What do you mean?'

But she was gone, with that glint in her eye and a smile on her face.

Joel called by. 'Hi Linda, make sure you're at the fellowship next week, won't you?'

'Sure, but why, Joel?'

'Ah! I'm sworn to secrecy! Just be there!'

And he too was gone.

A day or two later, Alethea showed up.

'Hey Linda, you will be there this week, won't you?'

'Yes, of course. But why is everyone asking?'

'Just checking you'll be there,' Alethea said. And she too was on her way.

There was a lot of anticipation in the prison as to what was happening at Prison Fellowship that week. It had been kept a secret, but we were all pretty sure there was going to be a special guest with us.

There were far more attending than usual that Thursday evening. The chapel was packed. Hugh, the Prison Chaplain, led the meeting as usual and then announced the guest.

'We have a real treat this evening. Please welcome Rita Nightingale.'

There she was. The lady that had been imprisoned in Thailand for drug smuggling. The one who wrote the book *Freed For Life*. The one who met two lady missionaries who led her to faith and then prayed with her for a pardon from her long sentence. So many parallels to me – and there she was!

We were transfixed from the beginning of her talk. Here was someone who knew what it was like to be on the inside, someone who could empathise with us, someone who spoke the same language.

I began to notice that the talk at the back of the room had slowed. Then it stopped. Everyone was listening.

Rita shared her story of how Christ had changed her life. There was an invitation at the end of the meeting for any to go to the front who wanted Christ to change their life as well. So many went forward. In fact, so many that I was asked to help pray with them. Such a privilege.

As I left the meeting that night, I was aware of someone in the shadows, following me. The moment I was on my own, there she was: Kelly. Slight panic. Fearful that I was about to be hit again.

'Meet me in the toilets on the south wing in five minutes.'

It was more of an order than a request. That's how Kelly operated. You tended not to say 'no'.

I was a little fearful, if I'm honest, but intrigued as well. As soon as we were in the toilets, Kelly blocked the door with a chair. What had I done? Why was she singling me out for punishment? I hadn't been the only one helping at the meeting...

'Can we talk, Linda? I need to know whether that lady was telling the truth. But I don't want anyone to see me.'

Kelly had a serious look on her face as she asked me to help her. Me? Help Kelly? That was a first.

'Yes, of course. Why don't you ask me what you want to know?'

'Well. I don't know. I mean, I'm not sure what to ask. I... I think I need to know God the same way as that lady. But... I'm afraid. I don't want anyone to see. I mean...' she smiled. 'I mean, it wouldn't be good for the image would it? To be part of the bloody God squad!'

I laughed. Slightly nervously. But I laughed.

Over the next thirty minutes, we talked, prayed and cried together. I had the privilege of leading one of the most hardened criminals I had ever met to a living faith in Christ. I wasn't imagining it – Kelly had a softer look on her face as she left the toilets that evening. And it wasn't long before she began to pluck up courage to tell others what had happened. Rather than being teased and bullied for the decision she had taken, many she spoke to also responded to the good news and prayed a prayer asking Jesus to change their lives. I guess they figured that if it could change Kelly so obviously, then it must be true!

'Well, Lord,' I said. 'I know I asked You to sort out the chatting at the back of the meeting. You really do know how to answer a prayer, don't You?!'

Release

It was a grey morning, but the birds were singing. As I walked away from the prison doors, it felt unreal. I was out. I found myself staring at the trees and flowers. They had been in short supply within the prison walls. So beautiful. How could anyone doubt God's existence when you saw their loveliness?

I had a ticket to get me back to Peterborough, but there were so many conflicting feelings at that point. I had only been in prison for eleven months, but I had become used to it. It felt like there were too many people on the streets. Too much rushing around. I found that my solitude in prison was not such good preparation for the hustle and bustle on the streets.

I told myself off. Not to be silly. In the end I got to the train and made it home. A nice surprise awaited me. Despite his earlier concerns about me, my landlord had repainted the flat for me and gave me free gas and electricity for a few days from another flat, until I could get reconnected. This really could be a new start.

Fitting In

Fitting back into church was a struggle. Pastor Michael had moved on and the new man was Pastor Gooden. Another lovely man, a little older than Pastor Michael, keen to help and encourage; but it wasn't quite the same with some of his Elders. A number were commenting on me being there, suggesting it wouldn't last. It made for a bit of an undercurrent and I wasn't sure I should stay around.

One Sunday, I was spoken to rather sternly by one of the Elders. Pastor Gooden was looking on in the distance with a slight frown on his face. The next Sunday he announced he was going to speak on winning the backslidden Christian back to Christ. As he spoke, he spoke of love, of going the extra mile, of encouragement and care. He spoke of the Father running towards his prodigal son. By the end of his talk, it was as if the whole atmosphere had changed. Gone was the judgement and attitude, replaced by people reaching out to me in love.

As I left the church building that day, I looked over to where Pastor Gooden was standing. He saw me. There was a smile and a nod in my direction. I'm sure I saw a twinkle in his eye.

I still had a strong desire for a man in my life. I wasn't fitting in to life outside without a man! It was what I had been used to. Returning from my brother Kim's wedding, having observed the new bride and groom, I found myself crying out to God for the right man. But emphasis on the *right* one.

'Lord, I've messed up big time in the partners I have chosen. I have to leave it to You. It has to be You that chooses, God, not me. But I do feel I need someone, Lord.'

Later that week, my future husband walked in to my life.

Ricky

I'd noticed Ricky around, but pretty well ignored him. But when a friend arranged for him to give me a lift home after a night out,

I couldn't but help notice him. Ricky was an athlete. He loved sports and his body showed it! Quite the good-looker, from a West Indian family, Ricky was a similar age to me and he seemed to be showing interest in me after that lift home.

Unlike other partners, Ricky took his time in dating me. He had a quiet faith in Christ, but had not been part of a church for a while. I invited him along, but he was put off on his first visit when someone suggested he would have to give up his running in order to attend church. Not the best of introductions.

He held back from attending church again and was hesitant to talk about his faith. I wanted a man who was going to go on strongly with his faith, so it was prayer time again...

'Lord, please will You sort Ricky out? I do feel he could be the man for me and I love the guy, so please can You sort it?'

I was unclear what sort of prayers you were meant to say for things like this. Should it be prayed 'in faith' and 'holding on to the promises' or should it be an 'if it be Thy will' type prayer? I wasn't sure. But I was content that God had things in hand.

A couple of months later there was a Christian conference I wanted to go to in London, but couldn't find anyone to go with. I felt God prompting me to buy two tickets.

'But who is the other one for, Lord?'

'Wait and see. I'll tell you.'

I was shocked when I felt I heard God telling me to invite Ricky.

'He won't come, Lord!'

I felt a slight reprimand from God. He reminded me of my prayers. Was He not to answer them after all? I guess I had assumed – or hoped – He might sort Ricky out without my involvement. But as is so often the case when we pray, God brings about a result that involves our participation.

'Yes, of course I'll come with you Linda.'

Well, well. That showed me the level of faith I'd been working at. I was delighted, of course. Even more so when Ricky responded in the meeting and re-committed his life to Jesus Christ. I saw him there with his hands in the air and tears rolling down his face. I felt God prompting me not to interfere.

'Leave him to Me, Linda, just leave him to Me.'

Later on Ricky explained what had happened. He'd seen a lady in the queue that was hunch-backed. He'd then seen her healed in the meeting. It was too much for him. He had to respond. God had done a new work in his life.

New Thinking

God was beginning to work in Ricky in a new way. And that meant that Ricky was beginning to see and think differently as a result.

It was dusk as we walked through Central Park in Peterborough. It had been a warm day and the walls and pathways had held on to some of the heat from the day. We sat on the grass, lying back, looking at the trees blowing gently in the evening breeze. I was trying to follow the flight of a couple of chaffinches as they darted in and out of one of the trees.

Ricky leaned forward on his elbow and looked at me.

'What? What, Ricky?'

He smiled. Said nothing.

Back in the car, he was looking right at me. And the look was serious.

'Linda. I really do love you, girl! Will you marry me?'

I had prayed, asked God to bring the right man across my path.

And how God had answered! We married at a Registry Office and then celebrated at a church service, which Pastor Gooden led. Just a small gathering, but so different to the rushed day with Terry.

Terry. Wow.

It seemed a lifetime ago now.

The abuse. The addictions. The prostitution. The drug trafficking. The prison sentence.

Another time. Another life.

As we walked out of the church building, I squeezed Ricky's arm and sent up a grateful prayer to a God who had abundantly blessed me and answered my prayers.

And a God who would need to answer more prayers as I began to face yet another challenge.

Chapter 10
Six Months To Live

By now I was working in the training section of a bank, based in their Northampton branch. It was a good job. There is no doubt that when you give your life totally to God and His purposes, He blesses back in abundance! However, there was something new to face coming my way.

One day I collapsed at work. It was totally unexpected; no warning, no pain. I just fainted. When I came round though, there was some pain. It was in my bowel area. I assumed it was a return of the old injuries caused by Sheridan, so went to hospital in good spirits, expecting that it would easily be sorted out. The initial diagnosis was that there was some sort of cyst. Nothing a small operation couldn't sort out. I should have noticed the frown on the surgeon's face.

I came out of the anaesthetic to find a number of people around my bed. Ricky was there. As were Paul and Kim, two of my brothers. Pastor Gooden was there too, looking serious.

I smiled. Tried to talk. But nothing came out of my mouth. No wonder – there were tubes everywhere. I noticed a Stoma bag by my side and began to panic.

'What's happened?' I tried to say. I looked around. I was in a side ward, but the main sign said 'intensive care'. Intensive care just for a small operation? What was this about?

A nurse arrived, apologising that the doctor wasn't there. The consultant arrived a couple of minutes later.

'Linda, it wasn't a cyst.'

'I guessed that, doctor,' I mumbled.

'Well, I'm sorry to say it was cancer. We have had to remove a large portion of your bowel. It's not clear if that will be enough. When you are recovered from the operation, we'll start you on radiation and chemotherapy to make sure we beat this.'

Stunned silence.

'Linda, you understand what I've said?'

I nodded. Still unable to speak clearly due to the tubes. I'm not sure I would have wanted to talk anyway. Had I gone through all these things only to get cancer? God, how could You do this to me?

Disbelief at first. Followed by anger. At God. At me for wasting my life. At anyone in sight! And slowly, acceptance. I had cancer. I didn't know if I could beat it. But it was no good just being angry about it.

I stayed in that hospital for three and a half months. I lost three stone in weight. The skeletal figure that was eventually allowed home didn't bear much resemblance to the seemingly healthy lady that had gone in.

Radiotherapy had finished and chemo had started. Thankfully, the Stoma bag had been temporary. It had been so hard dealing with that. I felt almost ashamed about it. Even today, I feel so much for those that have to use one all the time.

The treatment left me with brittle bones, at least temporarily. I had to walk with a stick – with a frame sometimes. Life had slowed to a crawl. Appointments. Doctors. More appointments. Treatment followed treatment. The chemo made me feel sick pretty much all of the time. At my worst moment, I was readmitted for a while and fed through a tube.

I was in a dream world. And not a good one. It was hard to look beyond the next appointment. Hard to understand what was happening. I was permanently tired, unable to do much other than sit down. My body ached. My mind was slow. There was a real world out there, but it seemed I had ceased to be part of it.

And then the conversation.

The Conversation

Further results had come back. The Consultant asked to see me.

'Sit down, Linda.'

Silence. He looked at his papers and then slowly at me.

'Linda, there's no easy way of telling you this. The cancer is still there. I don't think we can do much more other than keep you comfortable and out of pain. Linda, I don't think you will see another Christmas. You have about six months to live.'

My turn to be silent.

What little strength I had in my body seemed to evaporate into the warm day.

So that's it. Death.

Death in a sentence. I smiled to myself as I thought of the words I'd just used. Death in a sentence. The sentence of death.

I'd tell you more about that day, the day I heard the news,

but I can't. It seems my mind had blocked it out. I have no recollection of any further conversation with the Consultant. No idea as to what happened next, how I got home, who was with me even.

The treatment stopped. I settled in to a routine. Late to rise. Daytime television. Waiting for Ricky to come home from work. A snatched meal together. Early to bed while Ricky went out.

Ricky was taking it badly too. He drove the 80 mile round trip to Northampton every single day for all of the three and a half months. But now I was home, he wasn't coping.

'Ricky, why are you always going out? Why are you at the gym all the time? Spend time with me. I want to talk to you.'

He couldn't talk to me; that was the problem. He was hurting; wanting to take the pain for me if he could. But, of course, he couldn't. He hid his tears, tried to keep smiling. But his solution was to get out, workout, run at the athletics club. His way of trying to cope, knowing he could do nothing; not being able to deal with the thought of death.

The Doorbell

Not many people called after a while. I guess they didn't know what to say. Embarrassed perhaps. As Ricky had shown, not everyone coped with death the same way.

Pastor Gooden rang the doorbell at about 11.00 in the morning. He was still there two hours later. Two hours that would save my life.

Cup of tea in hand, he gave me one of those looks I had seen many times before. His way of saying 'pay attention, I've got something you need to hear'. And I did need to hear.

'Linda, why are you accepting this? Why have you just shut

down and decided to die? That's not the Linda I first met. Where's the fire gone? You've gone through so much. You have an amazing story. And He's still the same God! He hasn't changed. He's the one who saved you out of prostitution, from drug abuse, from alcohol ... You don't need to accept this!'

I felt myself beginning to cry, silently nodding my head as he continued.

'Are you going to listen to what a man says and just die, or are you going to believe in what God says? Linda, I really don't believe your time is up yet. You got more living to do, Missus!'

As he spoke words he had rehearsed before he rang the doorbell, I began to believe. As I sat there, I felt a new assurance that God knew, that He cared, that I could be well, despite what any doctor may say. I had accepted his words over me as a death sentence. But God spoke life!

That was it! God's sentence over me was words of life. Not a death sentence at all!

I could feel God's Holy Spirit working in me and through me as Pastor Gooden spoke the words. God was going to save me, heal me, and I, for one, wasn't going to accept this cancer any longer. As I listened to Pastor Gooden's words, the truth of God's Word was at work. A new strength entered my body. An empowering of the Holy Spirit.

A few minutes before, I could hardly stand without feeling tired. But as Pastor Gooden and I prayed together, I knew I was different. I got up without difficulty. The tiredness was gone. The sense of hopelessness was broken. I wasn't going to die! I knew it, just knew it, inside. I wanted to dance, to shout (I resisted while Pastor Gooden was still there!) God was going to heal me!

Ricky wasn't sure what had happened when he got home

from work that night. He was even more bemused, bless him, and even more tongue-tied. How do you cope with a woman that says she's dying when you leave for work in the morning and is then declaring God is going to heal her when you get back at night? He went to the gym. I don't blame him.

The Meeting

At that time, we were working as a church with other churches in Peterborough on what was called the 'JIM' campaign – 'Jesus in me'. Many of the church were going around, prayer-walking the streets of Peterborough and then knocking on doors, offering New Testaments and other literature. I wanted to do it too.

'Linda, you can't go. You're on crutches! Your bones are brittle. What if you fall?'

I went. Pastor Gooden assigned two people to help me and we walked and prayed the streets together.

My medical appointments were now at Addenbrooke's Hospital in Cambridge. Each time I went, I expected good news. Each time I came away disappointed, with different drugs offered me. Each time, by the time I got home to Peterborough, I was in faith again, knowing God was going to do something big.

Near the end of the JIM crusade, we had a visiting speaker from Canada. We all crowded into the church building and I was helped to my seat by Norma, one of my friends from church, along with Claudette, her daughter.

The preacher spoke of a healing God. He was sure God still healed today and at the end of the meeting, invited anyone to the front who wanted to receive healing.

Looking back, I wasn't at my best that night. It was a hot and crowded meeting and I had my crutches with me. I felt it was just too much for me to try and move, so I decided on this occasion to do nothing.

Norma nudged me.

Then again, harder.

Still not getting any response, she asked me outright why I wasn't going forward. I explained about the crutches and the number of people in the way, and the fact people were falling to the ground, which I couldn't do with my brittle bones, and so on. The next thing I knew, I was being carried to the front! Norma had grabbed me around the waist and, with Claudette's help, I was being propelled to the front of the meeting. I felt like the man on the pallet when his friends let him through the roof to see Jesus. There was nothing that was going to stop Norma and Claudette from making sure I got prayed for.

No one had told the speaker what was the matter with me. He looked at me, then at my crutches. 'Are you married to these?' he said and threw them to the side of the room.

The next thing I knew, he was shouting over me for the cancer to be gone! But no one had told him I had cancer.

'Lord, this is for real, isn't it?' I said.

As the visiting speaker continued to speak over me, I felt electricity go through me. It was as if I had been hit by a live cable. A sudden blast. I fell backwards, was caught, and lowered to the floor.

And then the strangest thing began to happen. I began to laugh. Uncontrollably. I just laughed and laughed! I don't think anything quite like that had been seen in these meetings before then and a number of the leaders weren't sure what to do.

'Leave her,' said the speaker. 'God is about His business. She's had a spirit of oppression on her life, but God is bringing a spirit of joy!' That night, I walked out without my crutches. I left them there. I never used them again.

The News

I went with some anticipation to my next Addenbrooke's appointment. Ricky dropped me off and went for a walk, agreeing to pick me up later. Tests were done and I was left waiting longer than usual.

The room was quiet; only one other patient waiting. My heart was beating faster. I prayed. This was the real test wasn't it God? This was the moment. You had spoken to me Lord. You had given me faith to be healed. You got me to that meeting. And even when I was unwilling, You brought Norma and Claudette along to sort me out! The prayer from the preacher. The power from the Holy Spirit. Electricity. Laughing. And now the results. Please, Lord, please...

Finally, the doctor came through and invited me into his office. As I sat down, he raised his eyebrows, creasing his forehead, as he looked at me over his glasses.

I swallowed hard.

'Well, Linda,' he cleared his throat. 'I'm not sure what has happened here or why it's happened, but the cancer has gone.'

'Pardon?'

'The cancer. It's gone, Linda. It's just shrivelled up and gone. Here, look at the x-rays.'

I was physically shaking as I took hold of the x-rays.

There in front of me was the evidence. No shadow. No stain on the x-ray. God had healed me.

Maybe I should have cheered and shouted. Maybe I should have cried. Or told the doctor that God had done it and that he needed to know God too.

But I did none of those things.

I smiled.

Just a smile; a contented smile. I leaned back in my seat, looked up to the ceiling. And smiled.

How amazing was my God!

The Letter

News travelled fast. My friends at church were so excited. Prayers were said. Cards were sent. Parties were planned.

And a letter was received from the hospital confirming the news. To this day, Pastor Gooden has the letter framed and on his wall. Testament to a God who heals. A God who has the final say on how long we each get to live. And for me, it was more than six months!

Chapter 11
A Past And A Future

I was hungry for more of a relationship with God. I loved the people at New Testament Church of God, especially the Pastor, but I felt I needed more. And I knew I had to find somewhere where Ricky would go. He'd not returned to church since being told he should give up his athletics. I know it wasn't the Pastor's fault, but the damage had been done and we needed somewhere new.

The Running Man

I often saw him run past our house in the Walton district of Peterborough. I didn't know who he was, but was soon to find out.

A leaflet had been posted through our door inviting us to some 'Prayer for Revival' meetings at Jack Hunt School. I felt prompted to go.

As soon as I arrived in the car park, I knew this was the place God was calling me to join. The welcome I got from the car park attendants was quite exceptional. Then again at the door. Even before the meeting had started, I felt at home. People came over to talk to me. They seemed genuinely interested in me, not just putting on a show. What was this place? How come they seemed so different?

Then the meeting began and, lo and behold, the running man stood up to speak. Pastor Dave Smith introduced himself and began to talk about a God who loved us, wanted the best for us, and had a passion for His Church. I'd never heard preaching like it. I was captivated by the words, challenged by the message. And home. I knew I was home, where God was calling me to be.

'Hello Linda! It's you!'

There in front of me was Norma. It seemed that she and Claudette had already made the move to this church. To see them there was a further confirmation for me.

KingsGate Community Church (called Peterborough Community Church in those days) has remained my home ever since. It wasn't long before Ricky started coming along. Hesitantly and occasionally at first, but nowadays, pretty much all the time.

As a church, we are long past hiring out schools now. Our own purpose-built facility, seating 1,800 in the main auditorium, opened back in 2006. On an average Sunday, at the time of writing, we get around 2,000 through the doors of Peterborough together with our sister church in Cambridge. And the guys on the car park are still exceptional!

'Linda, We Would Rather Have You!'

I was still reporting to Addenbrooke's every six months or so for further check-ups. All was clear for the first year, but then secondary cancer was identified in my womb. This was hard for me to take. I had believed for complete healing and here was more cancer, albeit, nowhere near as serious. And I had hoped for a baby with Ricky. We had lost a child in pregnancy early on in our marriage. I loved Ricky so much and even though I was 'getting on' a bit, I didn't want this further operation.

It took Janie Bingham, one of KingsGate's Staff Pastors, to speak sense into me. 'Linda, we would rather have *you* with an operation than lose you altogether!' Ricky was fine about it, of course, so more surgery was scheduled and a successful operation cleared me of the cancer. And all these years later, the cancer has stayed away.

I was sad though, not to be able to have a child. I felt God had promised me more children. But what I hadn't understood was how God's promise was to be fulfilled.

'I Just Need to Tell Them'

Although Georgie and Matt had been adopted so long ago, there was never a day went by when I didn't think about my children. I had first approached Social Services when I was ill with cancer, thinking that I should try and find my children before I died. But nothing came of it at the time.

I identified that the children must have been adopted in the Plymouth area as Terry had moved there shortly before he gave them up for adoption. I spoke to Jonathan, the head of the Plymouth Social Services department dealing with fostering. He asked why I wanted the contact.

'I just need to tell them that I love them and always will love them. I don't want them growing old thinking they have been rejected by their mother.'

Rejection can be so strong an issue in someone's life. Thinking you have been rejected by your own parents can cause a lot of harm. I wanted to somehow let them know of my love. Jonathan said he would do what he could. He needed me to work with someone from Peterborough Social Services, so this was arranged.

I began to pray.

A call to the Peterborough contact brought bad news. 'At this time, circumstances indicate that it will not be possible to proceed further.' Translated into English, this meant that Matt was still 16 and until he was 18 and able to make a decision himself, it would not be possible to contact either of them.

I continued to pray.

Persevering Prayer

Roll on two years and a lot of prayers later. With a prayer on my lips, I called the person at Peterborough on the day Matt reached 18.

'Hello, I don't know whether you remember me, but you said to call back when my son had reached 18.'

'Erm, yes. Yes, I remember. But I don't remember anything about calling back.'

My heart sank.

'What do you mean, you don't remember? I have lived by those words for two years! How can you say you don't remember saying it? "When he's 18, come back to me". That's what you said!' I was shaking with emotion and my voice was getting louder by the minute.

'I'm sorry, there seems to have been some misunderstanding. I regret I am unable to help you.'

More prayer.

I decided to consult a solicitor, who was willing to see me for free. She explained that it would always be the child who needed to contact the mother and not the other way around. But because I had once had cancer, there may be a way to reach the children, reflective of the illness possibly returning. I was grateful for any way around the situation, although I was positive that the cancer was gone, never to return!

Between us, we contacted Jonathan in Plymouth. He was astounded that nothing had happened.

'Linda, I'm so sorry you have not heard. Leave it with me. I promise I will come back to you.'

I carried on praying. It says in the Bible we need sometimes to be persevering with our prayer. Jesus tells the story of a widow that just kept on pestering a judge for justice, until he gave in. Jesus says that God the Father is not like that. He listens and responds. God honours persistence. And I was certainly persistent.

One day at work, I felt God prompting me to phone Jonathan.

'Linda! I was going to call you today. I've got news. It arrived this morning. You can't talk at work, can you? I'll call you this evening.'

He kept his word.

'There's good news and bad news, Linda. Which do you want?'

I asked for the good news.

'It's Matt. I've found him. He's written to you. The bad news is that he's in prison.'

Tears began to roll down my face. 'He's written to me. He's written to me! Oh Lord, he's written to me!'

Although the evening light was fading by this point, it felt like the sun was shining full into the living room. You could have added a heavenly choir and I would not have been surprised! My son. My son had reached out to me. All those prayers. Every day, thinking about him. And here he was, writing to me.

I tried to hold things together as Jonathan explained what would happen next. How our letters would have to go via him at first. And then if Matt wanted, he could write directly and invite me to see him.

I put the phone down, relieved, happy, elated. My son! I'd found my own son!

A minute later the phone rang again. It was Jonathan again.

'Linda, you didn't ask?'

'Ask what, Jonathan?'

'You didn't ask why he was in prison.'

'Jonathan, I don't need to. I don't care. I've found my son!'

As I put the phone down for the second time, I felt a prompting, a whisper from the Lord. 'Linda. That's just like Me. Just as your love for Matt is unconditional, so My love for you is unconditional. I love you no matter what. I always have. Always will. Even in the hardest moments. Even when you have gone your own way, done your own thing, I still love you. I love you Linda. I have always loved you. I will always love you. No matter what.'

I knelt on the floor. Persistent prayer turned to persistent worship.

The Dreams

Ricky came home from work. He could see something had happened.

'I know what it is, darling. I know what has happened,' he said excitedly. 'You've got a letter from Matt, haven't you?'

'But how do you know?' I was stunned. I hadn't had a chance to tell anyone.

'I dreamed it last night. I wasn't sure enough to tell you before work. But I felt God show me you were going to get a letter from Matt.'

I hugged him. Burst into tears again.

There are a lot of tears in this story aren't there? But these were tears of joy, of thankfulness to God. Not only did He find Matt for me, but He gave us an assurance in a dream that He was in charge.

Matt was in a young offenders institute in Aylesbury. A few days later as Ricky and I set out in the car. Ricky turned to me.

'I had another dream,' he said. 'I saw you meeting Matt. He looks just like your youngest brother Mark!'

'Surely not, Ricky. He'll look like his dad.'

'No. Like Mark. Wait and see.'

Ricky waited in the car as I stepped through the prison doors. And there was Matt. The last time I'd seen him, he was a baby. And here he was, all grown up. And looking the spitting image of his uncle Mark! The resemblance was uncanny.

We talked, cried, talked some more and, in the end, I left knowing a mother had found a son and a son his mother.

Matt also told me of Georgie. She too wanted to meet me and had passed a message on to Matt that she would be in touch.

As we drove back to Peterborough, the snow began to fall. Each snowflake different from the one before, all exclusively created by our amazing God. God had created a future for me. I saw each flake of snow as a blessing falling onto my life.

Undeserved, He loved me anyway. Despite my past, He was giving me a future. Every snowflake different from the one before; a varied, creative, anointed future. A special gift from the God who made each one different.

It was New Year's Day when the phone rang.

'Hello, can I speak to Linda please?'

'Yes, Linda speaking.'

'Linda... I mean, Mum. Hi. It's me. It's Georgie!'

I can't really tell you much about the conversation that followed. We were both crying so much, anyone listening would have been hard pushed to make any sense of it at all.

Georgie was married, living in London. Soon after I had the privilege of travelling down to meet her, her husband and the two children.

Grandchildren! As I hugged my daughter, I was so grateful that God had answered my prayers. That He had given me children after all. So many of them! As I write this, Matt is out of prison, married and doing well. And with seven children. Georgie now has four children. A Grandmother's blessing!

Terry

Our family story is not yet complete. Terry was to re-appear in a dramatic way. Georgie and Matt both wanted to try and find their dad if they could. I helped them with the date of birth and last known address. With a bit of detective work, he was found. And only just in time.

Terry was in hospital, in the final hours of his life, suffering with cancer. Matt called me. Would I come and visit?

Everything in me rebelled at the thought. But for the sake of the children, I went.

As I entered the ward and saw him in the distance, I became angry. I wanted to grab the pillow and smother him. I hadn't felt such anger for a long time. Overwhelming.

Unsure what to do, how I would respond, I got out. I found the hospital chapel and began to pray.

'Lord, I need Your help right now. I want to be able to pray with Terry; to help my kids with what they are facing. But I'm so angry! He really hurt me Lord! He tried to kill me! How can I let that go?'

Immediately, I felt God present with me. Gently reminding me of what every one of us did to His Son. How He had been abused to the point of death and beyond. How even then, He still loved us. We didn't deserve that love, but He gave it anyway.

If He had done that for me, given His Son, allowed Him to die for me, how could I not respond in love to someone who had abused me?

As soon as I thought it, I felt it. Incredible peace. There's no other explanation. It was God meeting me and helping me when I was too frail in my emotions to deal with it myself.

By the time Matt found me and asked me to return to the ward, I was ready.

There he was, Terry. Just the same. A bit thinner perhaps, and older of course, but so obviously Terry. The good looks were still there.

He was in and out of consciousness that afternoon, but I prayed with him every time he came around. 'Lord, meet him. Lord, forgive him and give him Your new life.'

It was still hard to pray a blessing on my abuser, but I did. And he knew it. From the depths of his sickness, he responded.

He could hardly speak, but was able to lift his hand. It went towards my neck. I pulled away. Was he still trying to hurt me after all these years?! But no, that's not what he meant.

He got a hold of the cross hanging around my neck, pulled it towards him and kissed it. Did God do something at that moment? I don't know. But what I do know is that with God's help, I had been able to let go of the hurt and the anger. I was free from the fear of manipulation, free of the fear of Terry himself. And as Terry held the cross, I prayed again; a prayer of blessing and release.

He died the day after.

A Moment in Time

God has been good to me, giving me moments in time when I have been able to deal with my past in more direct ways. Seeing Terry was not my only encounter of this type.

Toni called me to let me know a dear lady I knew in Southampton had died. I wanted to go to the funeral, but was pretty sure Sheridan would show up too.

With a lot of prayer and a lot of friends praying, I went. And there he was. The man who had enslaved me for six years of my life. I prayed again and went up to him.

After the surprise of seeing me, Sheridan listened as I spoke to him.

'I know you don't believe this stuff, Sheridan, but you need to know there is a God and one day you will be accountable to Him for all you have done. But He loves you. You can change. You should change!'

He smiled. Gave me a kiss on the cheek. And walked away.

I don't know what effect the words had. But I do know that at a moment in time, on one cold day in February, a drug lord, a modern slave owner and an abuser heard a message that could even then change his life. I pray it did.

Back to Prison

The same old steel doors crashed shut behind me as I walked into Holloway Prison. Snowy was there to meet me. She looked just the same after all these years. The same glint in the eye. As we walked through to the chapel, we were joined by Alethea. As small as ever, still giggling, and just as passionate about her faith.

We were there to help run an Alpha day. A large number of the inmates had signed up for the Alpha Course, an introductory course to Christianity. Part way through, there is an 'Alpha Away Day' where you learn about the Holy Spirit in particular. Well, you can imagine, can't you, the jokes that go around a prison on that one. An 'away day' indeed! Renamed a 'Home Day' due to certain circumstances.

I was introduced and began to tell my story. Abuse, alcohol, drugs, drug running, prison, cancer, completely healed, and completely changed by God. I noticed as I talked that the back few rows that had continued to talk at first, began to quieten, until eventually, they were listening to every word – as God the Holy Spirit began to do His work, bringing change and conviction. Later on in the day, I looked around at an amazing sight. We had invited all those with a faith who wanted more of the Holy Spirit to come to the front. Now there were around twenty-five 'bodies' laid out on the floor! As we had prayed for them, God had met them, baptised them in the Holy Spirit. They had fallen to the floor under the influence of the Holy Spirit and we now had the wonderful problem of what to do next!

It was a privilege to be there that day and it's a visit I have repeated. God is at work in the prisons of the UK.

Celebrating Recovery

God is at work in KingsGate too. One of the programmes we run is called Celebrate Recovery, for any and all who want to break harmful habits in their lives, or who are just feeling hurt and in need of healing. Working with my old friend, Janie, I have the pleasure of ministering to those on the course, helping them with their struggles and seeing them set free to a new life in God.

My story was told one Easter service to the whole church on the big screen. It helped a number there relate better to all that God was doing in their lives.

I remain involved with the poor and homeless too, working on the streets at night, offering food and prayer. And for my 'day job', I work for a housing association, helping many of the same people start again.

Don't get me wrong. It's not perfect. Ricky and I still have our occasional differences. And I still need loads of prayer for most things I've been through! But I never tire of telling my story. In the end it's the story of a gracious God who stepped into a life that was lost; a life facing death at every turn.

By God's grace, I have cheated death. With God's help, I am living life. Life as God planned. The best He has for me. I would have it no other way.

It's my story. But it's God's story too.

He has a story for you too, by the way. It's different from mine (you'll be glad to know!), but it's made perfectly for you to enjoy God's best.

A final scene. It was a Sunday morning at KingsGate and I was sitting in the coffee shop. Hundreds were filing out of the first meeting into the atrium. Hundreds more arriving for the next meeting. I'd just seen Claudette on the stage as part of the worship team. I saw Norma helping with the stewarding. Janie was chatting to some newcomers. And there was Ralph. He'd written a book recently. I wondered...

'Ralph, you know most of my story. I wonder: would you be able to write it down for me? It's just that I think there are people out there that may be helped if they read it.'

'Well,' said Ralph, 'we can give it a go.'

So we did.

A Letter From Linda

Dear friends,

Thank you. Thank you for reading this far. I hope and pray my story has been a blessing to you.

As I read back through the pages, it sometimes seems to be someone else's story. Not that these things didn't happen just as they are written, but it somehow belongs to another person in another age.

If God hadn't stepped into my life, I wouldn't have cheated death. I wouldn't be here to tell this story. I am living proof of a living God. A God who saves, changes and heals.

I remain cancer free and madly in love with my husband Ricky. We celebrate 25 years of marriage soon. I'm so glad I let God take over and choose the right man in my life!

I still work with Celebrate Recovery as one of the leaders. It's one of the great privileges of leadership, to see people respond to God's love, get set free, and find the very best God has for them.

God chooses to use me. How amazing is that?! An ex-junkie, former alcoholic, former prostitute and thief. I wouldn't choose me – but God does!

In the book of Proverbs in the Bible it says, 'Trust in the Lord with all your heart and lean not on your own understanding. In all your ways acknowledge Him and He will direct your paths.'

God keeps His promises. Always has. Always will.

Love and prayers,

Linda.

About The Author

Ralph Turner is a leader and director at KingsGate Community Church, Peterborough. He is responsible for International Mission and reaching business communities.

He works part-time in the pensions industry and was formerly International Pensions and Benefits Director for a number of multinational companies.

Ralph is married to Rohini and they have four adult children. You can find out more from Ralph's blog:

www.mountain50.blogspot.com